GERRYMANDERS

GERRYMANDERS

How Redistricting Has Protected Slavery, White Supremacy, and Partisan Minorities in Virginia

Brent Tarter

University of Virginia Press

CHARLOTTESVILLE AND LONDON

University of Virginia Press

Printed in the United States of America on acid-free paper

First published 2019

9 8 7 6 5 4 3 2 1

Library of Congress Cataloging-in-Publication Data

Names: Tarter, Brent, author.
Title: Gerrymanders : how redistricting has protected slavery, White supremacy, and partisan minorities in Virginia / Brent Tarter.
Description: Charlottesville : University of Virginia Press, [2019] | Includes bibliographical references and index.
Identifiers: LCCN 2019006667 (print) | LCCN 2019009062 (ebook) | ISBN 9780813943213 (ebook) | ISBN 9780813943206 (cloth : alk. paper)
Subjects: LCSH: Gerrymandering—Virginia. | Election districts—Virginia. | Political culture—Virginia. | Virginia—Politics and government.
Classification: LCC JK1343.V3 (ebook) | LCC JK1343. V3 T37 2019 (print) | DDC 328.73/0734509755—dc23
LC record available at https://lccn.loc.gov/2019006667

Maps by Nat Case, INCase, LLC

Cover design: David Drummond, adapting map of 1991 congressional districts by Nat Case

CONTENTS

ACKNOWLEDGMENTS

For reading an early draft and making valuable suggestions I thank:

Toni-Michelle C. Travis, professor of political science at George Mason University, a frequent commentator on Virginia politics and government, and editor of the *Almanac of Virginia Politics;*

J. Douglas Smith, of Colburn Conservatory, author of the prize-winning *Managing White Supremacy: Race, Politics, and Citizenship in Jim Crow Virginia* (2002) and of *On Democracy's Doorstep: The Inside Story of How the Supreme Court Brought "One Person, One Vote" to the United States* (2014); and

Jeff E. Schapiro, a political analyst who has written often about gerrymandering in his regular column for the *Richmond Times-Dispatch;* also

Richard Holway, acquisitions editor at the University of Virginia Press, who was enthusiastic about the project from the very beginning; and

Nat Case who prepared the maps.

GERRYMANDERS

1

THE GERRYMANDER MONSTER

This short book presents for the first time the full history of more than two centuries of the gerrymandering of legislative and congressional districts in Virginia. A gerrymander is a deliberate drawing of electoral districts to give an advantage to one political candidate or party, to influence who gets elected and who does not, and thereby to further or hinder the chances of particular public policies being adopted or defeated. Gerrymanders have taken place at all levels of government, from district lines for the election of members of Congress and state legislatures to city and county governing bodies, school boards, and judges in some states. Most of the scholarship on gerrymanders focuses on how gerrymanders have influenced which political party controls Congress, but gerrymanders of state legislative districts are arguably even more important. In most states, legislatures not only draw congressional district lines but also draw their own district lines as well as, sometimes, district lines for other elective bodies. Gerrymandered legislatures are therefore of the utmost consequence in local, state, and national politics and government. Gerrymanders affect our taxes, our public schools, and every other public policy decision.

Partisan gerrymandering to give one political party or group a long-term advantage is not essentially different from allowing changes in the rules of baseball to give the home team four strikes per out and four outs per inning but limit visiting teams to three strikes and three outs. Teams limited to three strikes and three outs could theoretically still win and occasionally would, but they would be at a serious and permanent disadvantage. The rules of baseball guarantee that both teams and all players have a free and equal chance to win by virtue of their skills. Partisan gerrymanders, however, disrupt or prevent a fair electoral process that should allow a majority of voters to elect the candidates who best represent their beliefs and interests. Legislators who draw electoral district lines are always the home team. That is what makes partisan gerrymanders extremely important and almost always unpopular except among the politicians who benefit from them. As is often said, in a representative democracy voters should select their representatives; representatives should not select their voters—but that has often been the case.

Just such an event led to the coining of the word *gerrymander.* It entered the English language on March 26, 1812, in a *Boston Gazette* article that showed that the peculiar shape of a new Massachusetts Senate district resembled a dragon, a salamander, or a "GERRY-MANDER." The new word for the "new species of *Monster*" included the surname of Governor Elbridge Gerry, a signer of the Declaration of Independence who was elected vice president of the United States later that year. His allies in the Massachusetts General Court (the state legislature) designed the district in hopes of retaining a Senate majority for their political faction.[1] The pronunciation of the word has since changed. Gerry's name was pronounced with a hard *g,* but the word for the practice is pronounced with a soft *g.*

In the 1907 book *The Rise and Development of the Gerrymander,* the first scholarly study of the subject, Elmer C. Griffith described the practice as "a political device" that "sets aside the will of the popular majority. It is a species of fraud, deception, and trickery which menaces the perpetuity of the Republic of the United States." The gerrymander, Griffith repeated, is a "corrupt

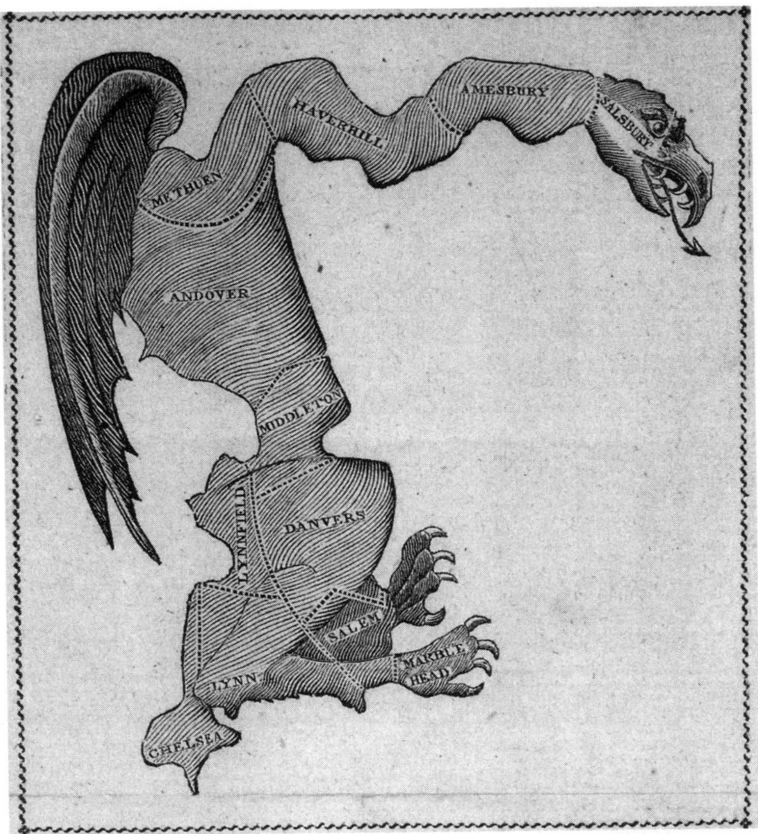

Fig. 1. Detail of a broadside that reproduced the March 26, 1812, *Boston Gazette* image and description of the original gerrymander. (Collections of the Massachusetts Historical Society)

form of legislation" that "stealthily seeks to destroy established principles of republican government."[2] Most definitions, like Griffith's, are pejorative and condemn gerrymanders as undemocratic and unfair. The definitions are all grounded on a bedrock belief that representative government requires a fair electoral process. They all reveal the difference between that popular belief and actual political practices. This is clearly evident in rulings of the

Supreme Court of the United States in the 1960s that required that the principle of one person, one vote replace centuries of political practices that had given some groups of people, regions, or interests advantage over others in voting and representation.

Gerrymanders have a long but overlooked history in Virginia. Legal scholars, political scientists, and journalists have written about several important episodes, but historians have largely ignored the subject, and nobody has connected to dots to see the larger picture and all its consequences. That is one purpose of this book. It is also intended to assist people who are not experts on this subject to understand the complex legal issues on the eve of the 2021 session of the General Assembly that will redraw district lines for the state Senate and House of Delegates and also for the U.S. House of Representatives.

In addition to the purely partisan purposes most people think of when they first encounter the word, gerrymanders in Virginia have protected special interests, such as those of landowners, slave owners, white supremacy, and minority rule. Virginia gerrymanders have taken many forms. Some have been very conspicuous, but some were almost invisible. Some have been obviously deliberate, but others appeared inadvertent. In redistricting, gerrymanders can operate at the micro level through subtle, small adjustments of one or a few district lines. In reapportionment, they can also operate at the macro level, such as constitutional conventions imposed on Virginia between the American Revolution and the American Civil War as well as in legislated schemes of representation in the state in the twentieth and twenty-first centuries. Many aspects of modern Virginia politics and the operations and consequences of redistricting and reapportionment appear in a clearer light when viewed in the context of colonial and nineteenth-century practices, but legal scholarship and judicial opinions usually omit or misrepresent the long historical context. In Virginia and elsewhere restrictions on the suffrage must also be kept constantly in mind (but are almost always ignored, too) because suffrage restrictions and apportionment schemes have worked in tandem to shape the state's political culture and the nature of its undemocratic politics and unrepresentative government.[3]

Redistricting, reapportionment, and gerrymandering have generated a large body of highly specialized technical scholarship. Some recent studies require advanced mathematical skills or a high degree of competence with computers to understand how politicians and their hired consultants analyze population data and records of voting patterns to manipulate electoral district lines. The legal scholarship and numerous complex court cases can also overwhelm or mystify people unfamiliar with legal research and writing. Hence the need for an explanation of the process and of the language used to describe gerrymandering for citizens who are not experts and need to understand this vitally important subject that affects the very essence of representative government. This book also includes citations to the relevant scholarship and to the leading case law for people who wish to read in more depth on the subject.

2

THE COLONIAL BACKGROUND

Prior to the American Revolution election laws in Virginia afforded no opportunities for gerrymandering legislative districts. The only regularly elected officials in the colony were burgesses who served in the General Assembly. Each was elected from a county, municipality, or chartered corporation so that there were no district boundaries to change. Colonial laws and practices that originated in the seventeenth century defined the suffrage and both embodied and created understandings about the nature of representation. Together those election laws and associated beliefs about representation laid the groundwork for the first deliberate gerrymanders (though not at the time so called) and criticisms of them in the nineteenth century.

At the meeting of the first General Assembly in 1619 two elected men attended from each of eleven principal settlements. The Virginia Company of London, which then managed the small settlements along the lower regions of the James River, authorized the governor, members of the Council of State, and the elected men to meet as a General Assembly to assist in governing the residents.[1] The assembly's journal identified the elected men as burgesses, a term that in England signified responsible men entitled to take part in municipal affairs.[2] Governor Sir George Yeardley's summons for the assembly stipulated that the burgesses be "Chosen by the inhabitants."[3] In 1624 Governor Sir Francis Wyatt directed that "all freemen" in each settlement select their burgesses "by pluralitie of voices."[4] It is highly unlikely that any but respectable free adult men—no indentured servants, no hired laborers, no enslaved people, and no women, children, or Indians—participated in the first elections. Only a small portion of the whole population took part.

From 1619 to 1643 the General Assembly was a unicameral legislature with the governor, members of the Council of State, and annually elected burgesses all meeting together. In the latter year the elected burgesses began sitting separately as the House of Burgesses.[5] Two years later the assembly authorized the free men in each county to elect four burgesses.[6] In 1661 the assembly reduced the number of burgesses from each county back to two.[7] (From time to time in the 1650s and 1660s some parish residents or vestries also elected burgesses, and the other burgesses seated them alongside members elected from the counties. From 1607 to 1786 parishes of the Church of England were part of the government of Virginia, and the government was part of the church.[8])

Comprehensive revisions of the colony's election laws in 1705 and 1736 retained the two burgesses per county rule and also allowed one burgess to the residents of Jamestown and authorized the president and professors of the College of William and Mary to elect one burgess by virtue of their holding a royal charter.[9] After charters incorporated Williamsburg in 1723 and Norfolk in 1736,[10] the General Assembly also allowed qualified residents of each to elect one burgess.[11] Allocation of seats in the lower house of the assembly remained almost unchanged from the seventeenth century until ratification in 1830 of the second state constitution.

A 1670 law limited voting to "freeholders and housekeepers who only are answerable to the publique for the levies"—that is, the law restricted the right to vote to taxpayers.[12] In 1684 the General Assembly confined the right of suffrage to "every person who holds lands, tenements or hereditaments for his owne life, for the life of his wife, or for the life of any other person or persons."[13] The assembly clarified the law in 1699 and declared "that no woman sole or covert, infants under the age of twenty one years, or recusant convict being freeholders shall be enabled to give a vote or have a voice in the election of burgesses."[14] The phrase "no woman sole or covert" excluded all unmarried, married, and widowed women explicitly, even though the word *freeholder* used in that statute to describe landowning people eligible to vote usually had a white, male connotation; and the disfranchisement of every "recusant convict" barred Catholics who refused to swear the oaths of allegiance and supremacy and take the test oath to deny the Catholic Church's doctrine of transubstantiation.

The election laws of 1705 and 1736 also required ownership of land as a prerequisite to vote. The 1736 law specified a minimum of one hundred acres of land or fifty acres of land and a house (or a lot or part of a lot in Williamsburg or Norfolk) in order to vote. In what was probably a unique colonial provision, the law allowed men who jointly owned a tract of land of the required minimum size to vote if they agreed on which candidates were to receive their votes.[15] The laws also allowed men to vote in and to be eligible to be elected from any county or city where they owned the minimum amount of land. (George Washington first won election to the House of Burgesses from Frederick County where he owned land, not from Fairfax County where he lived.) Those colonial precedents provided the models by which the government of the Commonwealth of Virginia functioned beginning in July 1776 and for many decades afterward.

A law the General Assembly adopted in the autumn of 1670 might plausibly, under an extremely loose definition, be classed as a proto-gerrymander. It combined into one county the two counties of Accomack and Northampton on Virginia's Eastern Shore, the peninsula between the Atlantic Ocean and the Chesapeake Bay. The region had been one county prior to being divided into two in 1663. In the words of the 1670 statute, "Whereas the late disturbances in the Counties of Accomacke & Northampton can by noe better meanes bee composed or settled than by reduceinge the Said Two Counties into one Itt is ordered that both the Said Counties bee united & Soe remaine one County untill there Shall appeare good cause againe to devide them."[16] The assembly's purpose in 1670 was not to alter or influence an electoral district but to deprive a haughty local grandee of part of his base of power, reduce his ability to exercise a disturbing influence, and so quell political unrest there. Colonel Edmund Scarburgh (also spelled Scarborough and several other ways) was then the largest landowner on the Eastern Shore, sometime sheriff of Accomack County, presiding judge of the county court, and a member of the House of Burgesses from the county. The 1670 law might have made it more difficult for him to win election to the House of Burgesses. The counties again separated into two without further legislative action in 1671 following Scarburgh's death, which activated the contingency clause in the law, "until there Shall appeare good cause againe to devide them."[17]

3

REPRESENTATION IN REVOLUTIONARY VIRGINIA

The Virginia Constitution of 1776[1] retained the two members per county apportionment of seats in the lower house of the General Assembly, which it renamed the House of Delegates, and created a new upper house, a Senate of twenty-four popularly elected members.[2] The constitution silently deprived the residents of the almost depopulated island of Jamestown of their one representative and the president and professors of the college of theirs. Following the legislative precedents of 1723 and 1736, the General Assembly later authorized qualified residents of the capital city of Richmond to elect one delegate beginning in 1789 and residents of the city of Petersburg to elect one in 1816.[3]

The colonial model provided the pattern for the new state government. Because every member of the lower house was elected from one county or city, county and city boundaries formed electoral districts, which left legislators no scope to alter electoral districts or to change the number of representatives to be elected from any jurisdiction. The Constitutions of 1830, 1851, 1864, and 1869 each created new House of Delegates districts that in some instances included more than one county or a county and adjacent city and therefore could be, and in 1830 and 1851 definitely were, contrived for a political purpose. In legislative redistricting from 1871 to 1971 Senate district boundaries always followed county and city boundary lines. With the exception of one court-ordered redistricting that was in force only for the year 1972, House of Delegates district boundaries followed county and city boundaries from 1871 to 1982. Prior to 1971, no district boundary line ever divided a city or a county.

Unlike districts for the House of Delegates from 1776 to 1830, district lines for the Senate could be manipulated from the beginning. A few minutes after the Virginia Convention of 1776 adopted the constitution on June 29, the president of the convention appointed Richard Henry Lee a committee of one to draft an ordinance "to lay off" the state into "districts for the choice of Senators."[4] No surviving records indicate what criteria, if any, Lee employed to draft the bill. He was a very busy delegate during the final few days of the convention and probably did not have time, even if so inclined, to find and consult any of the available tax records or tabulations of the number of militiamen in the counties. Those would have been the only sources from which he could have ascertained the approximate numbers of adult white males in the counties if he had intended—which we do not know—to divide the new state into twenty-four districts of approximately equal population. The convention amended and passed Lee's draft ordinance on July 4, 1776.[5] Each of the districts consisted of multiple counties, which for the first time created conditions in which gerrymandering by recombining counties into different configurations could potentially change the outcomes of elections. Until 1817 the General Assembly did not change the arrangement of Senate districts.

The creation of elected upper houses of assembly during the American Revolution precipitated in-depth discussions about the nature of representation. Who or what was it that representatives represented? Did they represent the men who voted for them, all the residents of the county or district, all owners of property who were the only eligible voters, or the political subdivision(s) from which they were elected? Who was entitled to representation?

And who should be entitled to vote for representatives? Those intimately interrelated questions were at the heart of the constitutional revolution that took place in the United States between independence in 1776 and ratification of the Constitution of the United States in 1788.

Residents of the colonies had modified practices that originated in England and devised their own ideas about the nature of political representation. In the British Isles in the eighteenth century only a small proportion of residents voted, probably a smaller proportion than in most of the North American colonies where all governments restricted the suffrage to owners of real property. Many people in Great Britain had believed that all the king's subjects were represented in Parliament by virtue of being the king's subjects—that is, they were virtually represented even if they had not voted, and even if men elected from their vicinity did not reside there. Each member of the House of Commons theoretically represented the whole realm. On the other hand, North Americans had come by the middle of the eighteenth century to associate legitimate legislative representation with particular localities in which representatives had personal interests and about which they had personal knowledge. No member of the House of Commons could ever possess that knowledge or have that interest in any colony, and in fact many members of Parliament had little or no knowledge of or interest in their own constituencies. Virginia burgesses, however, by law always had to own property and therefore possess a certain amount of knowledge about and interest in the county where they won election.[6]

Virginia election laws prohibited candidates from promising to support or oppose any particular measure,[7] so burgesses had not so much been thought of as representing their constituents but as being elected, in the British sense, to use their best judgment in the overall interest of the colony. The Revolution began to change that. By the time the word *gerrymander* came into being Americans in general and Virginians in particular believed that their elected representatives should represent their views and interests.[8]

The Convention of 1776 that adopted the first constitution for the Commonwealth of Virginia also adopted the first state declaration of rights. Section 6 of the Virginia Declaration of Rights stated that "all men, having sufficient evidence of permanent common interest with, and attachment to, the community, have the right of suffrage."[9] The colonial laws had in effect defined ownership of real estate as "sufficient evidence of permanent common interest with, and attachment to, the community." The Constitution of 1776 specifically endorsed and perpetuated that definition with its requirement that "The right of suffrage in the election of members for both Houses shall remain as exercised at present."[10] That thereby incorporated into the new constitution the 1736 election law (the statute in force "at present" in 1776), which allowed the vote only to free adult men who owned or possessed a long-term lease on at least one hundred acres of land or fifty acres and a house in the country or a lot or part of a lot in Williamsburg or Norfolk.

The requirement that men own land in order to vote had been virtually universal in the colonies, and most of the Revolutionary-era state constitutions retained it. Edmund Randolph, who was a member of the Virginia Convention of 1776 and also the first attorney general of the state and the first attorney general of the United States, later wrote, "That the qualification of electors to the General Assembly should be restricted to freeholds was the natural effect of Virginia having been habituated to it for very many years, more than a century. The members of the Convention were themselves freeholders and from this circumstance felt a proud attachment to the country in which the ownership of the soil was a certain source of comfort. It is not recollected that a hint was uttered in contravention of this principle. There can be no doubt that if it had been, it would have soon perished under a discussion."[11]

The property qualification therefore remained in force in Virginia under the Constitution of 1776 and in revised form under the Constitution of 1830 until ratification of the Constitution of 1851, seventy-five years after Virginia ceased to be a colony. Virginians made only one change to that requirement during the life of the Constitution of 1776. In 1785 the General Assembly reduced the freehold requirement from one hundred acres of land to fifty acres or twenty-five acres and a house and also made past practice into positive law and specifically excluded "free negroes or mulattoes" from voting.[12] The property qualification denied the vote to a large part—probably a majority—of adult white men and thereby politically privileged the class of adult, white, male landowners.

Under the Constitution of 1776, as during the century and a half of colonial precedent, Virginia's government was not in any sense democratic. In the limited sense that it was even representative it represented the class of tobacco planters and almost nobody else. As early as the middle of the seventeenth century the government of Virginia was a government of the tobacco planters, by the tobacco planters, and for the tobacco planters. Restrictions on the suffrage and distribution of representative seats secured their political dominance.[13]

What might have been the first deliberate Virginia attempt at a gerrymander took place shortly after the Revolutionary War, more than twenty years before the word was coined. Rumors circulated in Virginia late in 1788 that Patrick Henry and other men in the General Assembly who had opposed ratification of the Constitution of the United States were planning to draw electoral district boundaries for the new House of Representatives in such a way as to prevent James Madison and perhaps other advocates of the Constitution from winning election to Congress. Henry and his allies in the assembly had already elected two opponents of the Constitution, Richard Henry Lee and William Grayson, to the United States Senate and rejected Madison for that honor.

The rumors provoked public and private complaints about the propriety of what Henry and the others appeared to be doing. The language of some critics closely resembled language people used in and after 1812 to denounce gerrymanders. For example, "Decius" included in a long series of newspaper articles about current politics a sentence that exposed and condemned the rumored scheme. "Decius" characterized it as unfair and undemocratic, as critics of gerrymandering have always regarded the practice. "I call it an attempt to deprive the people of their choice of a Representative," "Decius" explained in language rather like that of Elmer Griffith more than a century later, "because the very idea of its being necessary to form a district in any particular way, to affect the election of any one, is sufficient evidence that the decision intended is contrary to the inclinations of the natural majority to be affected; and an attempt to form it so, is only in other words, to deny them the right of choosing for themselves."[14]

Some scholars doubt the accuracy of the allegations in part because evidence of motivation is scarce. Moreover, if the authors of this congressional district act[15] intended for it to bring about the defeat of Madison and others they failed. Madison and men who had supported ratification of the Constitution won majorities in six of the state's ten congressional districts. Even if the scheme had succeeded we would probably not now refer to henrymandering rather than to gerrymandering because the Fifth District in which James Madison and James Monroe opposed each other in the first federal election did not have such a bizarre shape as the 1812 Massachusetts Senate district. It was not and did not appear misshapen at all. In fact it would have been difficult to draw any congressional district lines that would not have put Madison into a district with some influential man or men who had opposed ratification of the Constitution.[16]

That Madison faced Monroe may later have given some added credibility to the charge simply because Monroe went on to be a

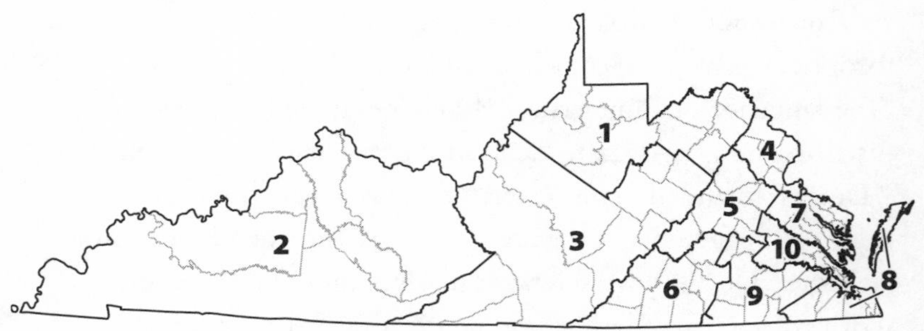

Map 1. 1788 congressional districts

governor twice and a senator, diplomat, secretary of war, secretary of state, and president. But Monroe was not then necessarily a more formidable opponent than some other men Madison might have run against. If Madison had faced some other opponent of the Constitution who did not become so famous later, however well known and influential he was in 1788, the configuration of the Fifth District might have appeared less deliberately contrived to bring about Madison's defeat. It is also of interest to note that Madison won election to the House of Representatives that year in part—perhaps in large part—because he appealed to Baptists in the district, who had opposed the Constitution because it did not adequately protect religious liberty. Madison promised to add a protection for religious freedom to the Constitution, which he did with his draft for what became the Bill of Rights.[17] That is one of the first public episodes that demonstrated that by the 1780s Virginians had come to believe that people they elected should represent their opinions and interests.[18]

In Elmer Griffith's 1907 study of early gerrymandering he suggested that the 1792 and 1813 Virginia congressional redistricting laws were in effect deliberate, small-scale gerrymanders. He based his surmises on a rather small body of evidence and the fact that a few members of Congress lost their seats in the next elections.[19]

4

A GERRYMANDER IN FACT THOUGH NOT IN NAME

The provisions of the Constitution of 1776 were not in any demonstrable way designed to favor any person, group, region, or interest other than landowners, but they nevertheless did. Thomas Jefferson exposed that in the 1780s in his *Notes on the State of Virginia.* He came out against the freehold requirement for the suffrage and proposed that representation in the assembly be in proportion to the number of voters instead of two delegates per county. In Jefferson's opinion representatives represented voters. The old rule had given a disproportionately large number of representatives to the small southeastern counties with relatively fewer white residents than elsewhere. Jefferson contrasted the effective electoral influence of voters in Warwick County (now a part of the city of Newport News) in the southeast, one of the smallest and least-populous counties, with that of voters in a larger and much more populous county. He calculated that on election day "every man in Warwick has as much influence in the government as 17 men" in the Potomac Valley county of Loudoun.

Jefferson estimated that collectively 19,000 eligible voters "living below the falls of the rivers, possess half the senate, and want four members only of possessing a majority of the house of delegates." (By the phrase "falls of the rivers," Jefferson referred to what is called the "fall line," the limit of navigation of deep-draft vessels, in shoal sections of the Potomac, Rappahannock, James, and Appomattox Rivers along a line running roughly south from a few miles above Alexandria through Fredericksburg, Richmond, and Petersburg to the North Carolina border.) Because eastern representatives who lived near the new capital city of Richmond were more likely to attend full sessions of the assembly than men who lived hundreds of miles away in the west, Jefferson argued, "These nineteen thousand, therefore, living in one part of the country, give law to upwards of thirty thousand, living in another, and appoint all their chief officers executive and judiciary."[1] At that time the General Assembly elected the governor, attorney general, treasurer, auditor of public accounts, and all other executive officers and all judges except county justices of the peace.

The numbers Jefferson cited were quite small, but he was writing about the minority of Virginians who voted, not the whole people who had to obey the laws legislators passed and pay the taxes lawmakers imposed on them. He regarded that as inherently unfair, a violation of the basic principles of representative government because it granted a minority of voters a majority of members of the legislature. Other people agreed. When western Virginians wrote a constitution for the new state of Kentucky in 1792 they expressly required that seats in the lower house of the legislature be "apportioned among the several counties according to the number of free male inhabitants above the age of twenty-one years in each."[2]

Jefferson's complaint about the discrepancy between the effective political influence of voters in Warwick County and voters in more populous counties was dramatic and durable. In 1816 a new generation of Virginians deployed his reasoning and revived his comparison to argue that the undemocratic situation he had described in the 1780s had grown worse. "If representation were equalized," several northern and western Virginia men who published a call for action declared in June 1816, "and Warwick county were taken as the standard by which the number of representatives from all the other counties should be regulated," the counties of Loudoun and Frederick "would be entitled to forty-five delegates each!" The men also pointed out that voters in the westernmost region elected far fewer members of the Senate than they would have been entitled to if seats in the two houses were then allocated solely according to population. "If he be asked," they concluded, "why so gross and flagrant an inequality of representation in the senate has been suffered to exist for so long—why a law has not been passed for new modeling the senatorial districts—the answer is an obvious one. The representatives of a minority of the people have the whole powers of government in their hands, and they will consent to no measure which has a tendency to transfer that power to its rightful owners, the majority. We say the rightful owners; for we presume it will not, and cannot, be denied, that it is a fundamental principle of our government, that the will of the majority should govern." In short, the men concluded, the Constitution of 1776 that gave two delegates to each county and the senatorial districts created at the same time had made "an absolute mockery of the principles of free government."[3]

Later that year about seventy men from nearly forty Virginia counties (none of them in the east) met in the Shenandoah Valley town of Staunton and formally petitioned the General Assembly to pass a law to enable the people to vote for members of a convention to revise the state's constitution. "No doctrine has received a more universal assent," they declared, "than that in a republican government, the will of the majority should be the law of the land. And yet in a state, boasting of the pure republican character of its institutions, this first and fundamental principle of republicanism, does not exist."[4]

In 1817 the General Assembly redrew senatorial district boundaries and simultaneously revised the rate of taxation on real estate in different parts of the state. Legislators did both in one law, which indicates how intimate politicians regarded the relationship between property ownership and representation in the legislature—in much the same way that their early laws and their constitution reflected an intimate relationship between property ownership and the suffrage. The new law made some minor alterations to four regions the assembly had created in 1782 in response to complaints about inequitable taxation of land, regions that had then roughly corresponded with the distribution of wealth—that is, of large valuable plantations and slaveholding—in the state.[5]

The provisions of the 1817 law revealed a gerrymandering intent. It divided the state into four regions that closely resembled the 1782 districts. The easternmost included all the area east of the fall line. That had always been the heart of the slaveholding area of old Virginia. The second included all the area between the fall line and the crest of the Blue Ridge Mountains. In that region by 1817 slavery was as important as in the east. The third embraced the valleys between the crest of the Blue Ridge and the crest of the Alleghany Mountains. Slavery was then relatively less important there than in either of the two eastern regions. The westernmost encompassed all the land west of the crest of the Alleghany Mountains. In most of that region slavery was of rather little consequence. The 1817 law reduced the number of senators from eastern Virginia and increased the number from the western region.[6]

In proportion to their numbers white men in the mountains and the west remained underrepresented in both houses of the General Assembly but to a somewhat lesser extent in the Senate than they had been. White residents of eastern and southeastern Virginia where the largest number of enslaved Virginians and owners of enslaved Virginians resided remained overrepresented in both the Senate and the House of Delegates. Even as the reapportionment partially redressed some western grievances, it guaranteed majorities in both houses of the assembly for voters in the region of Virginia with the largest population of slaves. That is to say, representatives represented property—slave property—slavery as an institution—as well as voters, citizens, or residents.[7]

5

THE GREAT GERRYMANDER OF 1830

Following more than a decade of almost constant public pressure for a convention to replace the Revolutionary constitution, the state's second constitutional convention met in the autumn of 1829.[1] The enabling law provided for the election of four members from each of the twenty-four senatorial districts.[2] Because of eastern domination of the General Assembly it apportioned seats in the convention so as to give a strong advantage to opponents of democratic reforms and allowed voters in the slave-rich eastern portion of the state to elect more delegates than voters elsewhere.

Members of the convention debated issues of the franchise and representation together. Advocates of universal white manhood suffrage, which was becoming the norm in much of the United States, pressed their case industriously but lost. Under the old ideas inherited from England, only adult white men who literally owned part of the country had "sufficient evidence of permanent common interest with, and attachment to, the community"—in the words of the Virginia Declaration of Rights—to qualify them to vote. The 1817 tax law that revised Senate districts strongly suggested that men elected to the legislature also represented that property as the source and guarantor of political rights. Should property in the form of land continue to be the only property taken into account in settling the basis of representation? Ownership of slaves as well as ownership of land conferred prestige and social stature on a person or family in post-Revolutionary Virginia. Owners of slaves had a conspicuous stake in the prosperity and stability of the state—in the status quo, in fact. Should owners of slaves be allowed to vote even if they owned little or no land?

Article III, section 14 of the Constitution of 1830 defined and limited the suffrage. It restricted voting to "Every white male citizen of the Commonwealth, resident therein, aged twenty one years and upwards" who met a revised property qualification. The word *white* was new to a Virginia constitution. Suffrage had been legally confined to males since 1699[3] and since an act of assembly passed in 1785 to "Every male citizen (other than free negroes or mulattoes) of the Commonwealth."[4] In practice, though, the word *freeholder* and other terms used to describe eligible voters before that time commonly had both male and white connotations.

A majority of convention members refused to abolish the requirement that adult white men own or hold a long-term lease on land in order to be able to vote. They nevertheless made an important change that in part reflected a different commercial understanding of property. Article III, section 14 required voters to own or hold a long-term lease on land worth at least $25 or be "a house-keeper and head of a family . . . and shall have been assessed with a part of the revenue of the Commonwealth within the preceding year, and actually paid the same."

If, as before, ownership of land remained prima facie evidence of what the Declaration of Rights defined as "evidence of permanent common interest with, and attachment to, the community," then the value—and $25 was a substantial amount of money then—rather than the physical extent of the property and payment of taxes on it became the new measures of the owner's right to take part in government.[5] And because the state imposed taxes on personal property in the form of slaves, owners of slaves could therefore count their value in claiming the right of suffrage under the new constitution. Other forms of untaxed property, such as ownership of a shop or business enterprise, shares of stock in a bank, canal company, or toll road, did not automatically confer the right to vote.

The convention scrapped the two delegates per county apportionment of the House of Delegates that dated back to 1661[6] and created what in hindsight I can accurately describe only as the Great Gerrymander.[7] Article III, section 2 required that the lower house consist of 134 delegates elected annually from districts distributed within the geographical regions of the 1817 reapportionment of the Senate—thirty-one delegates from west of the Alleghany Mountains; twenty-five between the Alleghany Mountains and the Blue Ridge; forty-two between the Blue Ridge and the fall line; and thirty-six from east of the fall line. (By west of the Blue Ridge the convention meant only, as its distribution of legislative seats demonstrates, the watersheds of the Shenandoah and South Branch of the Potomac Rivers, not the area immediately west of the crest of the Blue Ridge Mountains all the way south to the North Carolina border.) Section 3 enlarged the Senate from twenty-four to thirty-two members, "of whom thirteen shall be chosen for and by the counties lying West of the Blue Ridge of mountains, and nineteen for and by the counties, cities, towns and boroughs lying East thereof." Many of the House of Delegates districts encompassed two or more counties or a county and a city, but none of the district lines bisected a city or county.

The Constitution of 1830 increased the number of members of both houses to be chosen from west of the Blue Ridge, but it left voters east of the Blue Ridge able to elect majorities in both houses even though demographic data compiled for the members of the convention suggested that within a decade or two a majority of white Virginians would reside west of the Blue Ridge.[8] Article II, section 4 made the assignment of legislative seats according to the 1817 regional boundaries permanent. It declared, "It shall be the duty of the Legislature, to re-apportion, once in ten years, to wit: in the year 1841, and every ten years thereafter, the representation

Map 2. Regions described in the Constitution of 1830 for election of members of the state Senate and House of Delegates

of the counties, cities, towns and boroughs, of this Commonwealth, in both of the Legislative bodies: Provided, however, That the number of Delegates from the aforesaid great districts, and the number of Senators from the aforesaid two great divisions, respectively, shall neither be increased nor diminished by such re-apportionment." Section 4 also provided for representation for any new counties the assembly created but prohibited the General Assembly when doing so from altering the numbers of delegates and senators to be elected from each of the four "great districts" for the House of Delegates or the two "great divisions" for the Senate.

The new state constitution borrowed language from the Constitution of the United States for creation of districts for the election of members of the House of Representatives. Article III, section 6 ordered, "The whole number of members to which the State may at any time be entitled in the House of Representatives of the United States, shall be apportioned as nearly as may be, amongst the several counties, cities, boroughs and towns of the

State, according to their respective numbers, which shall be determined by adding to the whole number of free persons, including those bound to service for a term of years and excluding indians not taxed, three-fifths of all other persons."[9] Congressional district boundaries, like legislative district boundaries, followed city and county boundary lines until the 1970s. The requirement embraced in the words "apportioned as nearly as may be . . . according to their respective numbers" was the first constitutional or legal requirement in Virginia for an apportionment based on population. No Virginia constitution required anything comparable for General Assembly districts until the Constitution of 1970.[10]

Insertion of what was called the three-fifths clause into the new constitution was the first, even though oblique, recognition of slavery in a Virginia constitution. The clause dated back to the 1780s when Congress and the Constitutional Convention of 1787 had adopted compromises on issues relating to taxation and representation and devised the formula of "three-fifths of all other"—meaning enslaved—"persons." Because the fraction allowed representation to embrace both numbers of people and valuable property the three-fifths clause—"federal numbers" as members of the Convention of 1829–30 called it—had strong appeal to convention delegates from and voters in the slaveholding areas of the state for the obvious reason that it allowed fewer of them to elect the same number of congressmen as a greater number elsewhere.

On January 14, 1830, the convention adopted the constitution by a vote of 55 to 44. A majority of eastern members voted in favor of it, and a majority of western members voted against it.[11] Western men campaigned to defeat ratification of the constitution as energetically as they had worked to bring about the convention.[12] Soon after the convention adjourned former convention member Alexander Campbell from the northwestern panhandle wrote a series of long articles for the *Wellsburg Gazette* (which does not survive) in which he condemned the work of the convention. The *Wheeling Gazette* (which does survive) reprinted the articles. Campbell recounted the debates in detail to expose what he believed were the constitution's most egregious affronts to free white Virginia men who were not landowners or (especially) slaveholders. Among his numerous criticisms was that in the provision for drawing districts for the state's representatives in Congress, the convention had borrowed the three-fifths clause from the Constitution of the United States and thereby inserted the detestable institution of slavery into the Constitution of Virginia. "This is the secret of the whole matter," Campbell explained in his fifth essay. Eastern Virginians had treated western Virginians as "demi-slaves, or an Irish peasantry." Eastern Virginians, he warned westerners, "may by her Legislative power call us into the field" to put down rebellions of eastern slaves "or tax us at pleasure." He concluded with a relevant as well as rhetorical question, "Why, in the name of the five senses, should we be subjected to perpetual servitude if this be not the principle"—protection of the interests of slave owners—on which the new constitution was based?[13]

The Great Gerrymander gave permanent majorities in both houses of the General Assembly to the eastern part of the state where slavery was most important. Enfranchisement of men who paid taxes (such as urban dwellers who may have owned a few slaves but little or no real estate) probably increased the number of voters in the eastern part of the state. That, together with the requirement that the assembly employ the three-fifths clause to redistrict seats in Congress, guaranteed a hefty political advantage for the declining proportion of white men in the state who lived in the east and owned most of the state's slaves. As Campbell had charged in his newspaper essay, the constitutional convention deliberately and permanently tipped the balance of political power toward slaveholders. By rejecting universal white manhood suffrage and adopting the Great Gerrymander the convention rejected democratic reforms in order to protect and preserve slavery.[14] The Great Gerrymander of 1830 did not benefit any political party or faction, but it definitely benefitted the minority of eastern Virginia men who owned men, women, and children and profited from their work.

6

THE GREAT GERRYMANDER REVISED AND DISGUISED

Demographic, economic, and cultural changes during the second quarter of the nineteenth century fundamentally altered Virginia and brought about the important democratic reforms embodied in the state's third constitution, which voters ratified in 1851. The members of the convention who wrote it revised and disguised the undemocratic Great Gerrymander for the same reason members of the Convention of 1829–30 had devised it in the beginning, to protect slavery and owners of enslaved men, women, and children.

When voters ratified the Constitution of 1830, which guaranteed white voters east of the Blue Ridge permanent majorities in both houses of the General Assembly, white residents east of the Blue Ridge outnumbered white residents west of it by about 57,000. The 1840 census showed a white majority west of the Blue Ridge of about 2,000, but the 1850 census reported a huge increase of the population in western Virginia, which created a 90,000 white majority west of the Blue Ridge.[1]

Intense partisan politics created new political dynamics, rooted in part in the serious sectional divisions within Virginia that had been conspicuously on display in the Constitutional Convention of 1829–30. Competition for votes was intense. During the 1840s leaders of both major political parties came out in favor of universal white manhood suffrage. In part that was a simple quest for additional voters and votes, but it also reflected the new popular mood in the country. Most Americans, including Virginians, had come to believe that their political legacy, expressed in the language of liberty from the American Revolution, was a democratic politics in which all adult white men had an equal stake in the country and an equal right to participate in its government. That came to be called, rightly or wrongly, Jacksonian democracy. It fatally undermined the centuries-old belief that only men who literally owned part of the country were fully entitled to have any part in governing it.[2]

At the same time, the importance of slavery in the region between the Blue Ridge and Alleghany Mountains increased. Completion in the 1850s of the Virginia and Tennessee Railroad between Lynchburg and the Tennessee border at the town later named Bristol opened up commercial opportunities in the region. As the number and proportion of enslaved people increased, white people there more closely identified their interests with the interests of white Virginians farther east. So, too, farther north in the Shenandoah Valley.[3]

Owners of enslaved people remained worried that an increase of political power in the west or by men who owned few or no slaves posed serious economic threats. Easterners may have had legitimate concerns that non-slave-owning men might support higher taxes on slave property to reduce their own tax rates on other kinds of property and thereby make slavery economically unsustainable, even without intending to undermine the institution. For decades prior to the American Civil War, Virginians who owned few or no slaves often expressed resentment about tax policies that directly benefitted owners of enslaved laborers. The protection of slave property had many and often divisive repercussions throughout the state's (and the nation's) political economy.[4] Like some men elsewhere in the United States who reluctantly accepted universal white manhood suffrage, the class of slave owners in Virginia realized that they would have to rely even more than in the past on schemes of representation—what we now recognize as gerrymanders—to protect their special interests.[5]

A major sea change was in process at mid-century, though, which may not have been so conspicuous at the time as it soon became and is in hindsight. With the disappearance of the generations of Virginia men and women who personally recalled the Revolutionary language of liberty in the eighteenth century, so disappeared most of the antislavery sentiment that had been embedded in that language. During the 1840s and 1850s a majority of white men and women in Virginia gradually accepted a proslavery ideology, an accompanying proslavery theology, and a racist belief in the permanent, unalterable inferiority of people of African birth or ancestry. Lamentations about slavery as a necessary evil or an unfortunate inheritance from the past that could not safely be got rid of gradually gave way to open endorsements of slavery as good for everybody, including even enslaved people themselves. Some individual men and women remained opposed to slavery, but their opposition had become politically inconsequential by 1850, and it virtually disappeared from public discourse by 1860.[6] Those widespread beliefs seriously reduced the practical likelihood that any of the state's politicians would attempt anything overtly dangerous to the institution of slavery. Acceptance of slavery eliminated another of the principal objections to universal white manhood suffrage, that men who owned no slaves posed a threat to slavery.

Virginians apparently came late to implementing the political implications of white supremacy and white solidarity that acceptance of slavery as a positive good made possible. Well before the middle of the nineteenth century white people in the lower South had recognized and in their politics implemented those beliefs. Slavery made universal white manhood suffrage safe and acceptable, and universal white manhood suffrage made slavery safe and acceptable.[7] Virginia was one of the last states to abolish the property qualification for voting. Virginia's people and its political leaders were still thinking through the implications of universal white manhood suffrage in 1850 when voters elected members of the state's third constitutional convention.

Following the refusal of the General Assembly to redistrict in 1841 as the Constitution of 1830 required, angry men in several western counties and cities assembled and petitioned the assembly to call another constitutional convention.[8] Men in the mountain county of Greenbrier complained in August 1842 about the "grievances under which the people of Virginia labour, from the unequal, arbitrary and geographical basis upon which the representation of the state is founded." They signed a petition to the General Assembly that asked in firm language for the reapportionment the state's constitution required, but they then went much further. They declared that they could not "sanction any apportionment of representation, which is not based on white population or its equivalent," without clearly explaining what an equivalent could be.[9] In effect, they demanded abolition of the Great Gerrymander.

In every General Assembly session for the remainder of the decade legislators failed to redistrict or call a constitutional convention.[10] In March 1850 the General Assembly finally passed a law to provide for the election of 135 convention members from thirty-seven districts. As in 1829 the law favored the east. It was not based explicitly on the geography of the Great Gerrymander but on a combination of population and tax data that worked the same way. The assembly ascertained the size of each district and the number of members for each by adding to the population of white people in each city and county the number of dollars the residents paid in taxes on their personal property. Personal property included slaves—and slaves had a taxable value greater than that of all other classes of property except land combined—which strongly shifted the weight of regional representation in favor of the east. Convention members represented both white people and their property, so that voters in the region with more valuable taxable property had more influential votes than voters elsewhere with a lesser amount of taxable property. A member from east of the mountains represented fewer white people and more slave property than a member from the west, and a member from the west represented more white people and a lesser amount of property of any description than a member from the east.[11]

The House of Delegates passed the bill on February 16, 1850, by a margin of 78 to 42. On March 2, the Senate amended it to change the boundaries of two western districts and passed the bill 17 to 11. Two days later by an unrecorded voice vote the House of Delegates accepted the Senate amendment. At the same time the delegates defeated by a vote of 76 to 35 a motion that the whole subject be "indefinitely postponed."[12] That vote and the margins by which the two houses passed the bill suggest that about two of every five legislators opposed holding a convention at all or preferred no convention to one in which seats were allocated in such a discriminatory sectional manner.

Members of the convention adopted universal white manhood suffrage and thereby discarded centuries of English and Virginian beliefs and practices that linked suffrage to ownership of land.[13] They abolished ownership of property and/or payment of taxes as a prerequisite for the suffrage and brought Virginia more or less into line with practices in most other states.[14] The constitution ratified in 1851 also for the first time allowed voters to elect most public officials from governor all the way down to justices of the peace and clerks of court. It granted voters the right to elect all the state's judges and democratized the structure of state and local government. That in turn allowed more men to take part in local politics. Those conspicuous important reforms overshadowed the revision of the Great Gerrymander to protect slavery.[15]

The convention revised and disguised the Great Gerrymander. It omitted reference to the 1830 constitution's four regions for election of delegates and two for election of senators. The new apportionment in Article IV, sections 2 and 3, though, was also based on sectional considerations and was almost as beneficial as the old to voters in the eastern stronghold of slavery and almost as injurious to voters in the freer west. The new constitution created districts for the election of delegates and senators that strongly favored the eastern portion of the state where a large majority of slaves and owners of slaves lived. Depending on how some counties along the Blue Ridge are counted, the apportionment granted voters west of the Blue Ridge where about 55 percent of the state's white population lived a slim 4 or 5 vote majority in the 152-member House of Delegates but granted the 45 percent minority of white voters who lived east of the Blue Ridge a whopping 30 to 20 majority in the 50-member Senate. If the crest of the Alleghany Mountains rather than the crest of the Blue Ridge is considered the real dividing line between east and west, as in reality it was by 1850, the west fared almost as badly, with more than a third of all the state's white people allotted 49 of 152 delegates but only 11 of 50 senators.[16]

Convention members made that distribution of seats in the assembly temporary because they could not agree on a satisfactory permanent basis for representation. Three-quarters of a century after the American Revolution they still had not reached a consensus on what it was that representatives represented. In six paragraphs of more than eight hundred words Article IV, sections 5 and 6 required the General Assembly to settle on a principle for representation in 1865 and in that year and every tenth year thereafter reapportion both houses of the assembly in accordance therewith. If the assembly could not then agree, the new constitution required voters to select one from among four options, none including the number of white inhabitants or even the whole number of inhabitants as a sole basis for representation.

One option was to apportion seats in both houses on the number of voters in each county and city, called the "suffrage basis," meaning the number of adult white men who actually voted. Representatives would therefore represent voters. That option appeared to favor the western portion of the state at that time. If the demographic trends evident during the first half of the century continued that would probably be the basis voters would select in 1865 if the assembly with its eastern-dominated Senate did not first impose another.

The second option was to apportion the two houses on what the new constitution called a "Mixed Basis," that is, "according to the number of white inhabitants contained, and the amount of all state taxes paid, in the several counties, cities and towns." Representatives would represent white people and also their property. That was how representation in the convention was apportioned. It had clearly favored residents of the east over residents of the west and because of the very valuable taxable slave property would continue to do so.

The third option was to apportion the House of Delegates on the suffrage basis and the Senate on the amount of taxes paid. Delegates would represent voters, senators property. That would likely prolong regional antagonism or even create political paralysis on such profoundly important subjects as taxation, because owners of slave property could retain a larger representation in the assembly than their numbers otherwise allowed, and they could dominate the Senate.

The fourth option was to apportion the House of Delegates on the suffrage basis (voters) and the Senate on the mixed basis (white people and their property). That, too, could prolong regional conflicts.

None of the options allowed voters—adult white men—to select either the white or total population as the foundation of legislative representation. The constitution restricted voters to those four options in 1865, but only if the General Assembly in that year did not select a basis of representation and reapportion the state. The wording of Article IV, section 5 did not explicitly limit the assembly to those four options. The assembly could, for instance, choose to apportion either or both houses on the basis of the white population, which no doubt would have been welcomed in the west. The assembly could also settle on what convention delegates in 1830 had called "federal numbers" based on the three-fifths clause of the Constitution of the United States. Representation would then be determined "by adding to the whole number of free persons, including those bound to service for a term of years, and excluding Indians not taxed, three-fifths of all other persons."

Under the Constitution of 1851 with its revised and disguised Great Gerrymander and most of the apportionment options offered to voters in 1865, the Senate of Virginia became and would remain the impregnable fortress for the protection of slavery.

The Constitution of 1851 also contained several other important new protections for slavery. Article IV specifically mentioned slaves and slavery for the first time in any Virginia constitution. Section 19 placed in the new constitution a requirement based on an 1806 law that "Slaves hereafter emancipated shall forfeit their freedom by remaining in the commonwealth more than twelve months after they become actually free, and shall be reduced to slavery under such regulations as may be prescribed by law." Section 20 stated that the General Assembly could impose restrictions "on the power of slave owners to emancipate their slaves; and may pass laws for the relief of the commonwealth from the free negro population, by removal or otherwise." And section 21 declared, "The General Assembly shall not emancipate any slave, or the descendant of any slave, either before or after the birth of such descendant." The constitution provided new, unalterable protections for owners of slaves and for slavery and explicitly authorized the assembly to deport free black people and thereby whiten the free population of Virginia.

Article IV, sections 22 and 23 required equal, uniform taxation of personal property based on its market value with one very important exception eastern slave owners in the convention insisted on. The sections placed a cap of $300 on the value of slaves subject to the personal property tax. The rising market price of enslaved men, women, and children, driven by brisk demand in the lower Mississippi River valley, would have cost slave owners in Virginia much more in taxes than without the limitation. Without limitation, the General Assembly could have unintentionally ruined slave owners financially by taxing slave property at so high a rate as to make ownership of slaves unprofitable or a financially insupportable burden on owners. After all, the power to tax, as Chief Justice John Marshall had famously written in *McCulloch v. Maryland* in 1819, "involves the power to destroy."[17]

One feature of the apportionment section nevertheless suggests that members of the convention tried to create districts for the House of Delegates that contained roughly similar numbers of voters—at least in some regions with comparatively few slaves. As had the Constitution of 1830, the new constitution assigned the most populous counties and the cities of Richmond and Norfolk two or three representatives each and created single-member districts elsewhere that consisted in some cases of one county and in other cases two or more counties. But they could not fit all the counties into that pattern. "The counties of Lee and Scott" in southwestern Virginia, Article IV, section 2 specified, "in addition to the delegate to be elected by each, shall together elect one delegate." In effect, the voters of each county were to elect one and one-half delegates, one from their own county and together one from both. This was an innovation in representation in Virginia. Such a representative was called a floter. The origin of the term, which apparently arose in the United States in the middle of the nineteenth century, is unclear, but it may have arisen from the idea that the floterial district spread, flowed, or floated over districts each with its own separate representation.

The convention adopted a different scheme for the three small counties in the northwestern panhandle and for two other counties in the southern mountains. The same section directed, "At the first general election under this constitution, the county of Ohio shall elect three delegates, and the counties of Brooke and Hancock shall together elect one delegate; at the second general election, the county of Ohio shall elect two delegates, and the counties of Brooke and Hancock shall each elect one delegate; and so on, alternately, at succeeding general elections." The section also directed that at the first election voters in Russell County elect two delegates and in adjacent Tazewell County one, at the second election Russell County elect one and Tazewell County two, "and so on, alternately, at succeeding general elections."

Section 2 also authorized the General Assembly "upon application of a majority of the voters of the county of Campbell, to provide, that instead of the two delegates to be elected by said county, the town of Lynchburg shall elect one delegate, and the residue of the county of Campbell shall elect one delegate." That, however, the assembly never did during the lifetime of the Constitution of 1851.

Seventy-five years after Thomas Jefferson had written in the Declaration of Independence and George Mason had written in the Virginia Declaration of Rights that all men were created equal, universal white manhood suffrage in the Constitution of 1851 made all white men almost equal on election day; but the disguised Great Gerrymander continued to make voters in the slaveholding parts of the state more equal, as George Orwell's pigs would later say, than others.

In the portions of Virginia where slavery was much less important than in other regions the limitation on taxation of slaves became a grievance of major proportions, much as the weighting of representation in favor of the east had always been.[18] When northwestern Virginians wrote a constitution in the winter of 1861–62 for what was to become the new state of West Virginia,[19] they included a clear repudiation of preferential taxation for owners of slaves or any other property. "Taxation shall be equal and uniform throughout the State," Article VIII, section 1 of the West Virginia Constitution of 1863 stated, "and all property, both real and personal, shall be taxed in proportion to its value, to be ascertained as directed by law. No one species of property from which a tax may be collected, shall be taxed higher than any other species of property of equal value."

Moreover, Article I, section 7 of the West Virginia constitution guaranteed that "Every citizen shall be entitled to equal representation in the Government, and in all apportionments of representation, equality of numbers of those entitled thereto shall, as far as practicable, be preserved." Article IV, section 4 required that all legislative districts "shall be equal, as nearly as practicable, in white population, according to the returns of the United States census. They shall be compact, formed of contiguous territory, and bounded by county lines." Northwestern Virginians knew that the Great Gerrymander in the Virginia Constitutions of 1830 and 1851 and the preferential tax treatment of slave owners had seriously discriminated against them. Their experience living in a state that slave owners dominated led them to write a clear and mandatory constitutional provision for equal representation. They made certain that their new state government could never perpetrate anything like the Great Gerrymanders of 1830 and 1851.

7

DISFRANCHISEMENT REPLACES THE GREAT GERRYMANDER

The creation of West Virginia and the abolition of slavery during the Civil War destroyed all the reasons for the Great Gerrymander. The Constitution of 1864, which loyal Virginians wrote,[1] abolished slavery and created new Senate and House of Delegates districts for the new Virginia without the West Virginia counties. Article IV, section 6 omitted the complex apportionment provisions of the Constitution of 1851 and required that the General Assembly "re-apportion representation in the Senate and House of Delegates" every tenth year "from an enumeration of the inhabitants of the State." The constitution did not, however, go so far as West Virginia's and require that the state's legislative districts, like its congressional districts, be compact and composed of contiguous counties that contained as nearly as practicable equal populations. For the first time, though, the Constitution of the Commonwealth of Virginia allowed members of the General Assembly to represent the people or the voters in each of the counties and cities, not any local or regional interest or any property. The constitution also abolished viva voce voting and required that all voting be by ballot.

Article V, sections 2 and 3 of the post–Civil War Virginia Constitution of 1869,[2] which granted the right to vote to African American men, did not exhibit any prima facie regional or special interest desiderata in the districts it specified for election of delegates and senators. Section 4 required, "At the first session of the General Assembly after the enumeration of the inhabitants of the State by the United States, a re-apportionment of senators and members of the House of Delegates, and every tenth year thereafter shall be made." The Constitution of 1869 was the last to describe legislative districts. The Constitution of 1902, Article IV, section 43, and the Constitution of 1970, Article II, section 6, allowed the districts in existence at the time the constitutions took effect to remain as they were until the General Assembly altered them. Beginning with the redistricting acts for the two houses of the General Assembly in 1871 and the congressional redistricting act of 1872,[3] the General Assembly exercised full constitutional authority to draw or redraw legislative and congressional district boundaries.

Race replaced slavery in the center ring of the state's political circus after the Civil War. Restrictions on the suffrage instead of gerrymanders proved most effective in reducing challenges to elite white domination of Virginia's politics and government. Sixteen years after universal white manhood suffrage came to Virginia in the Constitution of 1851, African American suffrage came to Virginia. It began with the Act to Provide for the More Efficient Government of the Rebel States, sometimes referred to as the First Reconstruction Act, which the U.S. Congress passed over the president's veto on March 2, 1867. It created military districts throughout the South and authorized the commanding general of each to supervise the actions of state and local government officials. The law designated Virginia as the First Military District. Under the authority of that law and two other congressional mandates later that year,[4] both white and African American Virginians voted for members of a convention to write a new constitution for the state. Two dozen African Americans, about half of whom had recently lived in slavery, won election to the constitutional convention on October 22, 1867. Article III, section 1 of the constitution they helped write and that was ratified in 1869 enfranchised "Every male citizen of the United States, twenty-one years old" except men who refused to disavow their Confederate past, one year before ratification of the Fifteenth Amendment imposed African American suffrage on the whole nation.

White men who remained opposed to participation of African Americans in public life held majorities in both houses of the General Assembly in 1876 and submitted a constitutional amendment to the voters, who ratified it by a margin of 129,373 to 98,359 in November of that year. It required payment of a poll tax. The authors of the amendment intended to make it too expensive for poor African Americans to vote. The amendment also disfranchised men convicted of minor crimes.[5] What was sometimes called the "chicken-thief" amendment was based on a racist assumption that African Americans were inherently more dishonest than white people and that they often stole things like chickens that had almost no monetary value.[6]

The constitutional change, amounting to a mere twenty-eight words, had the desired effect. The number of voters declined by about 10 percent after ratification of the amendment and no doubt contributed to a reduction in the number of African American men able to win election to the General Assembly. Thirty African Americans had won election to the assembly in 1869 and from eighteen to twenty had won in each of the elections of 1871, 1873, and 1875; but only eight were able to win in 1877. A corresponding decline in the number of African American men elected to local offices was almost certainly another consequence of the amendment, which was adopted only two years after a constitutional amendment that had reduced the total number of elective local offices.[7]

The 1876 amendment deliberately placed obstacles in the way of African American voting, but soon thereafter the biracial Readjuster coalition of farmers and working-class people that included both Democrats and Republicans drew African American men back into politics. Readjusters promised to refinance payment of the public debt to reduce the principal and rate of interest in order to be able to restore adequate appropriations to the public schools. Readjusters won majorities in both houses of the General Assembly in 1879 and 1881 and imposed numerous important changes on Virginia's political culture and governmental institutions. They also proposed their own amendment to the constitution to repeal the poll tax as a prerequisite for voting, but it left in place the petty larceny provision. Voters ratified it on November 7, 1882, by a vote of 107,303 to 66,131.[8] African American voting and office holding probably never again reached the levels they had attained immediately after ratification of the Constitution of 1869, but throughout the remainder of the 1880s and in the 1890s African Americans provided enough votes for Republican Party candidates that Democrats believed themselves constantly under threat of another biracial working-class coalition that might succeed permanently at what the Reajusters had succeeded temporarily.[9]

Thereafter, rather than attempt to reinstate the poll tax to depress African American voting, Democrats changed the state's voting laws. In 1884 after Democrats defeated the Readjusters and won majorities in both houses, the General Assembly passed a new election law usually referred to as the Anderson-McCormick Act. It created new three-member electoral boards for each county and city and empowered the assembly to elect all the board members.[10] That gave the Democratic Party majority in the assembly a monopoly on who registered voters and conducted elections, and they used it to their partisan advantage.

The Anderson-McCormick Act produced widespread corruption. Candidates or political parties printed ballots with their names or the names of their candidates on them, and voters had to obtain ballots and carry them to the polling place and either place the ballots in the ballot box or hand them to an election official for that purpose. Ballots were often on distinctively colored paper or of different sizes, so everybody could easily see how everybody else voted. And election officials employed numerous means to influence the outcome of elections. They sometimes required that African Americans or known white Republicans stand in separate lines from white Democrats and either allowed all the Democrats to vote first or made certain that lines of African Americans moved so slowly that all the men were unable to vote before the polls closed. Counters of votes also sometimes cheated, altered official returns, destroyed ballots, or stuffed ballot boxes. Party workers of both parties sometimes resorted to public intimidation of voters, bribery, or violence to win elections. Some politicians bragged about the effectiveness of their nefarious techniques, but some other Virginia political leaders were embarrassed that under their voting laws electoral practices had become notoriously corrupt.[11]

Although the Anderson-McCormick Act somewhat reduced the influence of African Americans in public life it did not sufficiently suppress the Republican Party to guarantee easy victories for white supremacist Democrats. Therefore, in 1894 the General Assembly passed the Walton Act, which introduced the secret, or Australian, ballot. The state printed ballots with all the names of all the candidates for every office, and voters marked them at the polling place. That meant, without specifically requiring as much, that voters be able to read. Illiteracy among African Americans remained much higher in the 1890s than among white Virginians in spite of the introduction of the state's first statewide system of free public schools in 1870. The new ballot for the first time made voting secret, but like the old ballot it also encouraged corruption. The law required each voter to draw a line "through three-fourths of the length of the name" of every candidate he wished to vote against.[12] That provided Democratic vote counters leeway to decide that a voter had not quite drawn a legal line through enough of a Democratic candidate's name, which disqualified the

Republican's ballot; or that a voter had just barely drawn a legal line through a Republican candidate's name, which allowed the ballot to count and be counted for the Democratic candidate.

Some gerrymandering occurred at the local level as part of white supremacists' overall campaign to prevent African Americans from winning election to public office. As early as 1871 officials in the city of Richmond discussed increasing the number of wards and redrawing district boundaries so that none had an African American majority and therefore reduce or eliminate the chances that African Americans could win election to the city council.[13] In the 1890s the city council did redraw the boundaries to eliminate black-majority wards and guarantee that no African American candidates could win election to the council.[14] No available scholarship exists to document how widespread that practice may have been, but in the twentieth century at-large elections of city councils evidently became the norm, which made it more difficult for African Americans to win local elections, and in fact none did until after World War II and then only in a few isolated instances.[15]

All of which led to the Constitutional Convention of 1901–02, the principal purpose of which was to install constitutional barriers against African American voting so that Democrats did not have to cheat in order to win elections.[16] Article II, the suffrage article of the Constitution of 1902, which the convention promulgated without a ratification referendum, consisted of twenty-one substantial paragraphs and was longer than the entire Constitution of 1776. It created mechanisms by which administrative officials, who were largely immune from judicial review of their actions, could make it difficult or impossible for men to register and vote. The article required payment of a poll tax for each of three years preceding an election. That effectively excluded from the ballot box poor black men and also poor white men.

The constitution and laws passed to implement it also required each man who wished to vote to seek out a registrar and go through a complex process of registration and examination without any guidance from the registrar. That vested in the registrars extraordinary powers of discretion to determine a man's eligibility to vote. Registrars could legally hand a black man or a Republican a blank sheet of paper that the applicant had to fill out without assistance precisely as the law required. Registrars sometimes defied the law and assisted known Democrats to complete the registration forms. And registrars could demand that applicants satisfactorily answer any questions they posed to an applicant about the applicant's qualifications.

The law created electoral boards to oversee the conduct of elections and the certification of election returns. All of those officers except collectors of the poll tax were appointees of the local judge who in turn was elected by the General Assembly in which Democrats with white-supremacy beliefs had and expected to retain a more-than-comfortable majority. The complicated processes and the methods of selection of the men who oversaw the process gave explicit constitutional sanction to the partisan political manipulation of all voter registration and voting procedures.[17]

Members of the convention understood that they were devising a scheme of voter registration that could easily be applied for a discriminatory purpose. Alfred P. Thom, a corporate lawyer from Norfolk, stated as much when he observed, "I expect the examination with which the black man will be confronted, to be inspired by the same spirit that inspires every man upon this floor and in this convention. I would not expect an impartial administration of the clause. I would not expect for the white man a rigid examination. The people of Virginia do not stand impartially between the suffrage of the white man and the suffrage of the black man."[18] Republican Albert P. Gillespie, from Tazewell County, summed up the racist motivation of the majority well when he said that "the negro vote of this Commonwealth must be destroyed to prevent the Democratic election officers from stealing their votes, for it seems that, as long as there is a negro vote to be stolen, there will be a Democratic election officer ready to steal it."[19]

Section 30 also contained a provision designed to prevent African Americans from winning election in a jurisdiction with a majority black population. It allowed the General Assembly to impose "a property qualification not exceeding two hundred and fifty dollars for voters in any county or subdivision thereof, or city or town, as a prerequisite for voting in any election for officers, other than the members of the General Assembly." During the woman suffrage campaign in 1915 Attorney General John Garland Pollard, who had been a member of the Convention of 1901–02, explained to the president of the Equal Suffrage League of Virginia that the property qualification in section 30 would make the election of African Americans in black-majority localities impossible. The proposed enfranchisement of Virginia women, including black women, would not undermine the disfranchisement of African American men and allow black Virginians to win election to public office even in black-majority towns and cities.[20]

Carter Glass, a Lynchburg newspaper publisher and future congressman and senator, took charge of the drafting and passage of the 1902 suffrage article. He explained to the convention that its provisions would "not necessarily deprive a single white man of the ballot, but will inevitably cut from the existing electorate four-fifths of the negro voters. That was the purpose of this Convention." A member of the convention interrupted at that point and asked Glass whether he proposed to achieve that result by fraud or discrimination. Glass replied, "By fraud, no: by discrimination, yes. But it will be a discrimination within the letter of the law, and not in violation of the law." He may have paused a moment then, although the official record of the debates does not so indicate. But with the inclusion of an exclamation point, the man who recorded what came next indicated that Glass exclaimed, "Discrimination!" as if he suddenly realized that the question implied that discrimination was a bad thing. "Why," he explained, "that is precisely what we propose; that, exactly, is what the Convention was elected for—to discriminate to the very extremity of permissible action under the limitations of the Federal Constitution, with a view to elimination of every negro voter who can be gotten rid of, legally, without materially impairing the numerical strength of the white electorate."

Glass concluded his speech by proudly remarking that they had made a "fine distinction" that allowed them to evade the Fifteenth Amendment, which prohibited states from denying the vote to any man "on account of race, color, or previous condition of servitude." Instead, Glass boasted, they had disfranchised men because they possessed the "characteristics of the negro," which during the long debates he and other members of the convention had identified as ignorance, dishonesty, credulity, unreliability, and general incompetence—not to mention a thirty-five-year-long history of voting for Readjusters and Republicans.[21]

Registration and voting dropped precipitately as a result of the Constitution of 1902 and the laws adopted to implement it. In the 1900 presidential election 264,240 Virginia men voted; in 1904 a mere 135,867, a reduction in the whole number of votes of 48.6 percent. The Republican vote fell from 43.8 percent to 35.2 percent of the total. The number of white voters declined by about 50 percent, and the small number of remaining black voters declined by about 90 percent[22] and remained insignificantly small in all but a few communities until the 1960s. In spite of what Carter Glass promised, more white men than black men lost the right to vote as a consequence of the disfranchisement provisions he prepared and pushed through the convention. Because most of the white men were Republicans or were poor and could not afford to pay the poll tax or manage to defeat the complex voter registration process, the effect of the Constitution of 1902 was to reduce the Virginia electorate to a smaller proportion of the adult male population than at any time in Virginia's history and guarantee Democratic Party victories. Indeed, a smaller proportion of adult Virginians voted during the first half of the twentieth century than in any other state or nation.[23] The Constitution of 1902 reversed the most important democratic reforms the Constitutions of 1851, 1864, and 1869 had introduced.

During the first two-thirds of the twentieth century maintenance of white supremacy, racial segregation, and elite domination of public life were the primary preoccupations of the state's political leaders, much as defense of slavery had been during the first two-thirds (less one year) of the nineteenth century. Gerrymanders largely gave way to disfranchisement. Having made disfranchisement almost immune from legal challenges based on the Fifteenth Amendment, Virginia's elite white governing class under the stern direction of Harry Flood Byrd, who inherited control of the state's Democratic Party in 1922, dominated politics and state government without serious challenges until the middle of the 1960s. Adding the years after the defeat of the Readjusters in 1883 and 1885, that meant that the elitists who had eliminated many white voters from the rolls when they implemented their white-supremacist constitution and their successors dominated the state for about eighty years, almost one-fourth of its entire English-language history to that time. This is abundantly documented in a very large scholarly literature with no dissent and very little disagreement even on matters of detail.[24]

8

MALAPPORTIONMENT IN THE TWENTIETH CENTURY

Until 1970, Virginia constitutions contained different provisions for reapportioning seats in the General Assembly and in Congress. For the assembly, the constitutions required periodic redistricting but specified no criteria, for the House of Representatives clear criteria but no requirement for how often. Article VIII, section 121 of the Constitution of 1902 did require a rough equality of population in wards if voters in cities with bicameral councils elected members from wards rather than at-large.

Each of Virginia's constitutions beginning with that of 1830 required the General Assembly periodically to reapportion seats in both houses of the legislature. Until the Constitution of 1970 none included any criteria for reapportionment or a requirement to design electoral districts for the assembly that were composed of compact and contiguous territory that contained "as nearly as is practicable" equal populations, as required in the state's constitutions since that of 1830 for congressional districts. The Virginia Supreme Court of Appeals took judicial notice in 1932 in *Brown v. Saunders* that "for a period of more than 102 years, the principle of practical equality of representation in the House of Representatives in Congress has been the fundamental law of Virginia."[1] That was not quite correct, however, both because of the distortions of the three-fifths clause before the Civil War and the failure of the assembly to redistrict after several census returns disclosed major shifts in population within the state.

That all the state's constitutions except those of 1776 and 1851 required legislative reapportionments after each federal census appeared to suggest that population was the primary criterion on which legislative as well as congressional representation was based. That is not quite correct, either. The 1851 requirement was not substantially different from the requirements of the previous or subsequent constitutions. Article IV, section 5 of the Constitution of 1851 required reapportionment at ten-year intervals beginning in 1865 instead of 1861, and Article IV, section 37 authorized the assembly to collect population statistics and tax data for the purpose. But for three-quarters of a century protection of slavery had seriously distorted legislative representation. Moreover, the General Assembly refused to exercise its constitutional responsibility to reapportion the two houses of the legislature in 1841; the death of the Constitution of 1851 as a casualty of the Civil War in 1865 meant that the revision of the terms of representation it required in 1865 could not and would not be done; and the Constitution of 1869 superseded the Constitution of 1864 before the latter's required reapportionment could take place. Consequently, even though it appeared from reviews of language in the state's constitutions that legislative reapportionments had regularly occurred beginning in 1841, in fact they did not begin until 1871.

University of Virginia political analyst Ralph Eisenberg therefore incorrectly concluded in an important 1961 summary of Virginia apportionment practices in the *University of Virginia News Letter* and in a 1966 article in the *Washington and Lee Law Review* that population had always been recognized as the basic principle for Virginia's legislative as well as congressional apportionments.[2] That basing representation on population did not equate to equality of representation also appears to have escaped his notice. Eisenberg and other commentators did not know about and therefore missed the consequences of the Great Gerrymander of 1830 and its disguised revision in 1851, and they failed to perceive how the three-fifths clause had in fact destroyed the requirement for equality of population in representation in the House of Representatives. But he and they did not miss the consequences for the twentieth century.

Accelerated urban and suburban population growth in eastern Virginia that began before and continued after World War II changed the proportional relationships among the regions of the state and also among the cities, counties, and towns in Virginia. The population increased most pronouncedly in the crescent-shaped region that stretched from the suburbs of the District of Columbia in northeastern Virginia, through the capital region with Richmond at its center, to the cities of Portsmouth, Norfolk, Newport News, and Hampton in southeastern Virginia. During the 1950s that region became relatively more populous, and consequently the old legislative and congressional districts based in part on earlier demographic patterns became imbalanced to the disadvantage of residents of the urban and suburban regions throughout Virginia but especially in the east.[3] At mid-century representation in the General Assembly of Virginia was definitely out of alignment with the ideal of equality, although by some criteria less out of alignment with recent population changes than in some other states.

The 1952 regular session of the General Assembly—from 1852 to 1866 and from 1880 to 1970 the assembly regularly met only in even-numbered years—did not redistrict the Senate and House of Delegates as the state constitution required. Byrd organization leaders in the assembly did not want to relinquish any of the advantages the malapportionment permitted them to enjoy. That deeply disturbed Alexandria delegate Armistead Lloyd Boothe, who obtained from Attorney General J. Lindsay

Almond an official but nonbinding ruling that the assembly's failure to obey the constitution's mandate was unconstitutional. Boothe compiled and circulated to members of the assembly, the state chamber of commerce, the League of Women Voters, and numerous Virginia newspapers a thirty-three-page handbook that detailed the malapportionment that then existed. Revising the comparisons Thomas Jefferson had made in the 1780s, Boothe complained, "Exact equality is impossible, but it is the basis of our democratic government that representation be equal. In a democracy some citizens should not have seven votes, other citizens five votes, and still others only one vote apiece. Yet that is the situation in Virginia today." He counted each vote in multimember districts as a multiplied vote. "Through the medium of the State Senate many of our citizens actually out-vote others 5–1. Through the medium of the House of Delegates many citizens out-vote others 7–1." Ultimately, Boothe persuaded large majorities of both houses of the assembly to petition the governor for a special session, which met in December and redrew legislative district lines so as to reduce some of the disparities.[4]

Political scientists and other scholars have devised various means to measure such imbalances. One method of analysis ascertained the minimum number of voters required to elect a majority in each house of a state legislature. By that measure and based on 1950 census data 43.93 percent of Virginians could elect a majority in the Senate, and 43.69 percent could elect a majority of the House of Delegates. Of the forty-eight states, Virginia then ranked ninth on a scale of best to worst for the Senate and sixth for the House of Delegates.[5] By 1960, though, because of demographic changes, 37.7 percent could theoretically elect a majority of senators, and 36.8 percent a majority of delegates.[6] Another method of analysis measured population differences between the least- and most-populous districts. During the 1950s the difference between the populations of the least- and most-populous

Senate districts rose from 17.6 percent to 29.93 percent and for the House of Delegates districts from 15.4 percent to 31.30 percent.[7]

A third method, which Paul Theodore David of the University of Virginia devised, sought to ascertain the effective electoral influence of voters, not unlike what Thomas Jefferson had tried to estimate in the 1780s and Boothe in 1952. David compared the number of inhabitants in each legislative district with the ideal average computed by dividing the population of the whole state by the number of members of each house, and from that determined the extent to which each person was underrepresented or overrepresented. If every delegate represented exactly the same number of citizens, the ratio would be 1 to 1. By that method, as Ralph Eisenberg summarized the calculations in 1961, "the value of the vote for delegate in underrepresented Alexandria before 1960 was .54. Meanwhile, the overrepresented Botetourt and Craig county citizen had a vote valued at 1.73. Similarly for the Senate, the voter in Arlington County possessed a vote valued at only .61 but the voter in overrepresented Culpeper, Fauquier, and Loudoun counties possessed a vote valued at 1.49." Statewide analysis of legislative representation by that method disclosed that the seven most heavily populated counties and cities of the state at the beginning of the 1960s were "significantly underrepresented with a vote valued at .73 while the most sparsely populated units are overrepresented with a vote valued at 1.24."[8]

None of the calculations appears to have taken into account the consequences of the disfranchisement of a very large majority of the state's African Americans completed in and after 1902 or the consequences of the simultaneous disfranchisement of a large proportion of the state's white people. The disfranchisement guaranteed minority rule in Virginia as a whole. Calculating over- or under-representation from census data minimized the actual reduction in the effectiveness of some votes and the increase in the effectiveness of other votes. Overrepresentation in the General Assembly for rural and small-town Virginia and underrepresentation for urban and suburban Virginia amplified the influence of the minority. An even smaller minority dominated politics and government in the region of Virginia with the largest population of African Americans and the smallest percentage of white Virginians—in southeastern Virginia, which had been the stronghold of slavery in the eighteenth and nineteenth centuries and was the most important and reliable stronghold of white supremacy and the undemocratic Byrd organization during the twentieth century. A portion—in some instances only a small portion—of a minority provided enough votes to elect members of the General Assembly. In the 1956 session of the assembly that required closing of public schools under federal court orders to desegregate, the twenty-one senators who voted for the law may have represented fewer Virginians than the seventeen senators who voted against it.[9]

Because so few Virginians of either race actually voted during the first two-thirds of the twentieth century we should pause to consider again, as Virginians had considered during and after the American Revolution, who or what elected representatives actually represented. Members of the General Assembly represented districts in a legal and technical sense but not necessarily the interests or beliefs of the people who lived there or even of a majority of them. It is doubtful anybody would have argued that legislators who supported "massive resistance" to desegregation of the public schools in the 1950s represented the opinions or interests of very many of the African American residents of their districts or even of all of the white residents. In a real political sense it would be more accurate to describe those senators and delegates as *un*representatives. They represented and defended the principles and practices of white supremacy. They represented Jim Crow. Restrictions on the franchise and malapportionment operated together as a twentieth-century Great Gerrymander to allow the undemocratic Byrd organization to continue to dominate state politics and government.

Deliberate, inadvertent, or neglectful manipulation of electoral districts political leaders in Virginia created during the twentieth century was immune until the 1960s from legal challenges in state and federal courts. Only two apportionment cases—one of them comparatively inconsequential—arose in Virginia before that decade.

Four years after the 1880 census the General Assembly redrew Virginia's congressional district lines to create a tenth district with an evident intent to increase the number of Democrats to be elected.[10] John Sergeant Wise, the incumbent at-large Readjuster/Republican congressman who thereby stood to lose his seat, contested the law, not on grounds relating to political fairness or gerrymandering, but rather on the grounds that it had not received the constitutional majority required in the Senate to override the governor's veto. In *Wise v. Bigger* the Virginia Supreme Court of Appeals relied on the authority of the journal of the Senate to establish that the law had been properly enacted. The judges remarked in passing, "The laying off and defining congressional districts is the exercise of a political and discretionary power of the legislature, for which they are amenable to the people, whose representatives they are."[11] The court did not claim or disclaim authority to pass on the legal propriety of the apportionment and left the subject to the General Assembly, but the judges' words clearly indicated that they did not believe that intervention into reapportionment or redistricting was a proper judicial responsibility.

In 1932 in *Brown v. Saunders* the Supreme Court of Appeals nevertheless ruled that the congressional redistricting act adopted earlier that year[12] violated the requirement of Article IV, section 55 of the Constitution of 1902 that the "districts shall be composed of contiguous and compact territory containing, as nearly as practicable, an equal number of inhabitants." The 1930 census had reduced Virginia's representation in the House of Representatives from ten members to nine.[13] Rather than redraw all the congressional boundaries in the state, members of the General Assembly ignored the requirement of the state constitution and combined two districts and shifted a few counties from the combined district to another. Each district should have included approximately 269,092 inhabitants, but the new district had 67,562 more than that, and another had 85,158 fewer. Without stating what "practicable" divergence from the equal ideal was permissible, the judges declared, "The inequality is obvious, indisputable and excessive. No argument is needed. It is demonstrated by the statement of facts." That the law conflicted with the constitution "is not open to reasonable controversy." The law was unconstitutional prima facie—or on first view or on the face of it—without requiring any analysis. Because less than one month remained between the date of the court's decision and the 1932 congressional election, the court ordered that for that one year all the candidates for Congress be elected at large.[14] As an unintended consequence, the state's only Republican congressman lost in the Democratic Party landslide that year, so the new law and the court decision, even without so intending, worked to the advantage of the Democratic Party.

9

THE REPRESENTATION REVOLUTION OF THE 1960S

Because Virginia's constitutions included no criteria for drawing legislative district boundaries comparable to the requirements for congressional districts, state courts had no obvious constitutional standard that could enable them to ascertain whether any legislative apportionment or redistricting act could violate the state constitution; no clear constitutional provision existed to violate. Federal courts also refrained from taking cases involving apportionment and redistricting laws in the states until the 1960s. Article I, section 2 of the Constitution of the United States contained no explicit requirements for how states should draw boundaries for congressional or legislative districts. Redistricting was very much a political act in which legislators sometimes sought political advantage for their party or faction; sometimes tried to guarantee their own reelection; sometimes tried to preserve traditional natural boundaries such as rivers or mountains in order to protect regional interests; or sometimes (as in Virginia) relied on county and city boundaries to preserve communities of local interest. Federal courts had no obvious mandate to interfere or authority to suggest or impose changes. In *Colegrove v. Green* in 1946 the Supreme Court of the United States declared that federal courts had no jurisdiction in cases that involved the highly charged political process of redrawing a state's congressional district boundaries. The majority in *Colegrove v. Green* resolved to stay out of what it called a "political thicket" in which courts had no business.[1]

On March 26, 1962, however, a badly divided Supreme Court ruled in *Baker v. Carr* that federal courts would no longer remain out of the thicket. The decision was purely a jurisdictional one that enabled people to challenge apportionment and redistricting laws in federal court on the grounds that district lines that had been drawn in ways that diluted the effectiveness of some votes might violate section 1 of the Fourteenth Amendment that prohibited states from denying "to any person within its jurisdiction the equal protection of the laws." Gerrymandering that allowed some voters to elect more representatives per capita than others could violate the requirement for equality that had been added to the Constitution of the United States in 1868.[2]

The Supreme Court plunged into the political thicket. In 1963 in *Gray v. Saunders* the Court declared that in elections for members of state legislatures any scheme that gave voters in one place more influence in an election or more representatives than the same number of voters in another place was a constitutionally unacceptable denial of equality and violated the Fourteenth Amendment. The Supreme Court declared that the essence of representative government required election laws and practices to be based on the principle of "one person, one vote."[3] The ghost of Thomas Jefferson should have been pleased.

Chief Justice Earl Warren's majority opinion in the influential June 1964 case *Reynolds v. Sims* spelled out the implications of the rulings in *Baker v. Carr* and *Gray v. Saunders* for all electoral districts. "The right to vote freely for the candidate of one's choice," the chief justice declared, "is of the essence of a democratic society, and any restrictions on that right strike at the heart of representative government. And the right of suffrage can be denied by a debasement or dilution of the weight of a citizen's vote just as effectively as by wholly prohibiting the free exercise of the franchise." Warren further explained at length that practices that allowed more-influential votes to some people than others or that gave representation to regions or interests were no longer to be regarded as constitutional. "Legislators represent people," Warren argued, "not trees or acres. Legislators are elected by voters, not farms or cities or economic interests," even though in many states, including in Virginia, that had in fact long been the case. Before the Civil War some voters had elected members of the General Assembly who in effect represented and protected real estate ownership or the special interest of slavery, and in the twentieth century a majority of legislators represented only a small minority of the population who insisted on racial segregation and disfranchisement of African Americans. "As long as ours is a representative form of government," the chief justice continued, "and our legislatures are those instruments of government elected directly by and directly representative of the people, the right to elect legislators in a free and unimpaired fashion is a bedrock of our political system."[4]

Warren acknowledged in *Reynolds v. Sims* that different constitutional requirements for one person, one vote operated on congressional and state legislative districts. The requirement in Article I, section 2 that "the People" elect members of Congress and the requirement in the Fourteenth Amendment that states treat all residents equally meant in practice that congressional districts must conform as closely as possible to the ideal of equal numbers in every district in each state. But the particular constitutional relationships between state legislatures and local governments that had no counterpart in the relationship between the federal and state governments could allow states the right to employ other criteria that might permit or even require wider variations from the equal ideal the Fourteenth Amendment required. "A State may legitimately desire to maintain the integrity of various political subdivisions," the chief justice explained, "insofar as possible, and provide for compact districts of contiguous territory in designing a legislative apportionment scheme." Reasons that might justify variations from the equal ideal could also differ from state to state. "Single-member districts may be the rule in one State," he continued, "while another State might desire to achieve some flexibility by creating multi-member or floterial districts. . . . So long as the divergences from a strict population standard are based on legitimate considerations incident to the effectuation of a rational state policy, some deviations from the equal population principle are constitutionally permissible."[5] Warren and the other justices did not provide any clear guidance to states about how much such considerations could allow states to deviate from perfect one person, one vote representation or define "rational state policy." In June 1964 the Supreme Court deliberately left it to future political negotiations and litigation to find answers to those questions.

In several other 1964 cases—*Wesberry v. Sanders, WMCA v. Lomenzo, Maryland Committee for Fair Representation v. Tawes, Davis v. Mann, Roman v. Sincock,* and *Lucas v. Forty-Fourth General Assembly of Colorado*—in one in 1968—*Avery v. Midland County, Texas*—and in one other in 1970—*Hadley v. Junior College District of Metropolitan Kansas City*[6]—the Supreme Court required that apportionments of elected representatives at all levels of government, from seats in Congress to city and county governmental bodies, be substantially equal on the basis of one person, one vote.

The opinions of Chief Justice Earl Warren in particular but also those of other members of the Supreme Court resembled the language of earlier generations of Virginians who had complained about the unfair apportionment of the House of Delegates under the Constitution of 1776, the ordinance of the Convention of 1776 that created electoral districts for the Senate, the 1817 hidden gerrymander of the Senate, and the Great Gerrymander of 1830 and its 1851 revision. Those nineteenth-century Virginians and the twentieth-century judges based their beliefs and rulings on principles of representative government as they understood those principles, not on legal or traditional political practices of long standing. The ideas eventually eroded and overturned centuries of political and legal practices and precedents.

Baker v. Carr in 1962 began a profound and widespread revolution in American representative government. The revolution continued during the 1960s with an amendment to the Constitution of the United States, several other decisions of the Supreme Court, the Voting Rights Act of 1965, and a new Virginia state constitution that together tossed legalized disfranchisement into the dustbin. In the short space of less than a decade those changes produced the most consequential and far-reaching alterations in voting and representation in American and Virginian history.

The Twenty-fourth Amendment to the Constitution of the United States, which was ratified in January 1964 (the General Assembly of Virginia did not ratify it), declared, "The right of citizens of the United States" to vote in all federal elections "shall not be denied or abridged by the United States or any State by reason of failure to pay any poll tax or other tax." In March 1966 in *Harper v. Virginia State Board of Elections,* which combined two lawsuits separately initiated in Virginia, the Supreme Court declared that imposition of a poll tax as a prerequisite for voting in any election abridged the right to vote that the Constitution of the United States guaranteed to every adult citizen.[7] Those two actions destroyed the poll tax that for more than half a century had denied the vote to thousands of African Americans in the South and to poor white people in Virginia.

On August 6, 1965, President Lyndon B. Johnson signed the Voting Rights Act.[8] Under authority of the Fourteenth and Fifteenth Amendments, it imposed restrictions on states with prior histories of racially discriminatory voting laws and practices, including Virginia, to prohibit electoral practices that denied or effectively diluted the votes of ethnic minorities. The law required that before any changes in state voting laws, registration procedures, voting practices, or electoral districts could take effect they first had to be approved by the Department of Justice or by the United States District Court for the District of Columbia. The law also required the attorney general of the United States to file a brief amicus curiae (literally, a friend of the court argument) in the then-pending case *Harper v. Virginia State Board of Elections* against the power of states to impose a poll tax as a prerequisite for the franchise. Federal supervision of state electoral practices under the Voting Rights Act became an even greater intrusion of federal power than the Supreme Court decisions into the traditional power of states to regulate election practices.

In 1970 Virginians ratified a new state constitution.[9] In many respects it brought the state into compliance with the mandates of the Supreme Court and the Voting Rights Act. The new constitution omitted the poll tax requirement and the complex and difficult registration procedures that had been in the state's constitution and laws since 1902. Article II, section 6 declared, "Members of the House of Representatives of the United States and members of the Senate and of the House of Delegates of the General Assembly shall be elected from electoral districts established by the General Assembly. Every electoral district shall be composed of contiguous and compact territory and shall be so constituted as to give, as nearly as is practicable, representation in proportion to the population of the district. The General Assembly shall reapportion the Commonwealth into electoral districts in accordance with this section in the year 1971 and every ten years thereafter."

Together, all those changes ushered in an era of increased voting by African Americans and poor white men and women, reminiscent in a number of ways of the short-lived democratic politics the Constitutions of 1851 and 1869 had introduced to Virginia for the first time a century earlier. The changes fundamentally altered the constitutional and legal contexts in which legislators redistricted or reapportioned congressional, legislative, and local governing bodies thereafter.[10] As some students of gerrymandering predicted, those several reformations in American law revived the partisan gerrymander as a political tool to accomplish objectives that in some instances disfranchisement and malapportionment had previously promoted or protected.[11]

10

THE REPRESENTATION REVOLUTION IN VIRGINIA

Almost every redistricting law the General Assembly enacted after the representation revolution faced a serious challenge in state or federal court. Even one of the important 1964 federal court cases that defined the representation revolution, *Davis v. Mann,* arose in Virginia hard on the heels of *Baker v. Carr.* In 1962 the General Assembly redistricted the Senate and House of Delegates and reduced but did not nearly eliminate the differences between the least- and most-populous districts in both houses.[1] The redistricting marginally increased the minimum number of voters who could elect majorities in both houses and marginally reduced the disparity between rural districts and urban and suburban ones. Significant differences remained, however, and several northern Virginia legislators filed suit in federal court as the months'-old ruling in *Baker v. Carr* allowed. In *Mann v. Davis* a three-judge panel of the federal court for the Eastern District of Virginia ruled 2 to 1, on November 28, 1962, that the differences in population between the least- and most-populous districts were so large that they were constitutionally impermissible. The judges ordered that unless the General Assembly in the meantime passed acceptable redistricting laws the senators who were to be elected to four-year terms in 1963 would have to run for reelection in 1965, because it would be intolerable to allow senators elected in 1963 from unconstitutional districts to serve until their terms expired at the beginning of 1968. The court allowed time for the General Assembly to enact new redistricting laws but retained jurisdiction to issue another ruling if necessary. One judge dissented in part because the variations from the equal ideal in the Virginia redistricting acts were not so great as in some other states and also because the earliest decisions of the Supreme Court on the subject provided inadequate guidance to determine what was and what was not permissible.[2]

The state appealed, and the Supreme Court scheduled argument of the case, then styled *Davis v. Mann,* with several other important apportionment cases for November 1963. In the interim some residents of Norfolk joined the original plaintiffs in the suit. Chief Justice Earl Warren delivered the opinion of the Supreme Court on June 15, 1964, at the same time the Court ruled on *Reynolds v. Sims* and the other cases. For the majority Warren declared, "Neither of the houses of the Virginia General Assembly . . . is apportioned sufficiently on a population basis to be constitutionally sustainable" and remanded the case (sent it back) to the three-judge district court.[3]

In accordance with the Supreme Court's ruling, the three judges required in September 1964 in the second ruling in *Mann v. Davis* that if the General Assembly did not enact a constitutional redistricting law the senators who had been elected in 1963 would have to run for reelection in 1966.[4] In November 1964 the General Assembly passed new redistricting laws that increased the number of legislators from the urban and suburban areas that had experienced the largest population growth since 1950 and reduced the variation between the least- and most-populous districts in the Senate from 2.65 to 1 under the 1962 act to 1.37 to 1, and in the House of Delegates from 4.36 to 1 down to 1.53 to 1.[5]

The following year in the final ruling in *Mann v. Davis* the federal court for the Eastern District of Virginia altered a provision of the 1964 redistricting law that had placed Shenandoah and Page Counties in a House of Delegates district with Rockingham County and the city of Harrisonburg. Under the 1964 law, residents of the four jurisdictions together elected one delegate, and the residents of Rockingham County and Harrisonburg elected another. The judges believed that the residents of the counties of Shenandoah and Page were thereby underrepresented and ordered that voters in the city and the three counties together elect two members of the House of Delegates.[6]

At the same time the judges also heard but rejected two complaints concerning the new eight-member district consisting of Henrico County and the neighboring city of Richmond, in which all the delegates were to be elected at-large. Some Henrico County residents complained that the 35.9 percent of the district's inhabitants who lived in the county would be unable to elect county residents, and some African Americans in the city complained that they would be unable to elect African American candidates from the large and populous white-majority district. In the combined district African Americans constituted only 29 percent of the whole population, but if the city and county were separate districts, African Americans in the city would constitute 42 percent of the population and have a better chance to elect black candidates. The judges refused to break up the multimember district into single-member districts, deferring to the long history of multimember districts in Virginia. They also added, "The concept of 'one person, one vote', we understand, neither connotes nor envisages representation according to color. Certainly it does not demand an alignment of districts to assure success at the polls of any race. No line may be drawn to prefer by race or color," only that no line be drawn that devalued any vote.[7]

Also in 1965, the Virginia Supreme Court of Appeals ruled that under both the state and federal constitutions the state's congressional districts contained unacceptably large variations in population. The General Assembly had declined after the 1960 census to redraw the ten district boundaries created in 1952.[8] By the 1960s the old districts were badly out of balance. The urban Second District in southeastern Virginia contained 25.0 percent more people than the ideal average, and the suburban Tenth District in northern Virginia contained 33.3 percent more; at the same time the Fifth District in rural southern Virginia contained 17.6 percent fewer people and the largely rural Seventh District in northwestern Virginia contained 20.9 percent fewer—a total population variance of 54.5 percent. In *Wilkins v. Davis,* the Supreme Court of Appeals declared that the districts the 1952 law created violated Article II, section 55 of the state constitution for the same reason as it had invalidated the 1932 congressional districting act (incontrovertible and excessive inequality) and also because the 1952 law violated the Fourteenth Amendment's principle of one person, one vote. In August 1965 the General Assembly passed a reapportionment act that reduced the variations among the districts to a range of between 4.5 percent below and 6.1 percent above the ideal average, a 10.6 percent variance.[9]

The 1971 redistricting laws for the state's congressional districts and its legislative districts based on the 1970 census were the first enacted under the revised state and national constitutional and legal requirements. Those laws as well as annexations of adjacent suburban neighborhoods the cities of Petersburg and Richmond undertook at about the same time produced important court decisions based on federal court rulings that specified more precisely the requirements of one person, one vote and the new Voting Rights Act.

In the 1971 congressional redistricting act,[10] the General Assembly reduced the population disparities among the state's ten congressional districts that demographic changes in the state produced since the previous redistricting in 1965. Democrats, who had large majorities in both houses of the assembly, used the occasion for partisan advantage. They shifted Montgomery County and the city of Radford from the Sixth Congressional District to the Ninth to put two incumbent Republican congressmen in the Ninth District. That might make it easier for a Democrat to win against a different Republican in the Sixth District in the 1972 congressional elections. They also placed the two Republican congressmen who then represented the Eighth and Tenth Districts in northern Virginia in the same district, potentially opening up another improved opportunity for a Democratic candidate there. They configured the Fourth and Fifth Districts south of the James River so as not to put two incumbent Democratic congressmen in the same district. The new Fourth District was long and narrow so as to include at its western end the Appomattox County residence of Congressman Watkins Abbitt. As seen in map 3, the shape of that district probably could have been found a prima facie violation of the state constitution's requirement for compact districts, as the 1932 redistricting act had been on the basis of equality of population, but it was not. The resulting variation in the populations of the districts ranged from 3.4 percent above the ideal average to 3.9 percent below, a range of 7.3 percent.

On March 1, 1972, the federal court for the Eastern District of Virginia ruled in *Simpson v. Mahan* that the disparity between

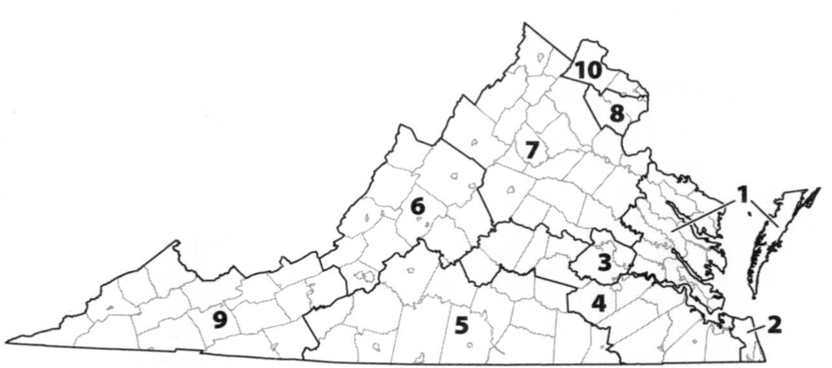

Map 3. Congressional districts created in 1971

the most- and least-populous districts was too great and directed the General Assembly to redraw district boundaries within ten days.[11] By then, Richard Poff, one of the southwestern Republican congressmen, announced that he would not run for reelection (that same year the governor appointed him to a vacant seat on the Supreme Court of Virginia), and William Lloyd Scott, one of the northern Virginia Republican congressmen, announced that he would run for the United States Senate. In addition, Watkins Abbitt announced his retirement. Therefore, when the General Assembly passed a new congressional districting act a few days after the federal court invalidated the 1971 law, the partisan motivations that had in part dictated the redistricting no longer applied. The 1972 law reduced the population disparity down to 0.68 percent.[12] That was well below the 3.1 percent variance the Supreme Court in 1969 in *Kirkpatrick v. Preisler* had found unacceptably large for Missouri congressional districts.[13] As map 4 shows, the new Fourth and Fifth Districts were also very differently shaped than the original districts.

The 1971 acts that drew new districts for the Senate and House of Delegates also faced legal challenges under the one person, one vote rule.[14] These laws created fifty-two single-member, multimember, and floter districts for the election of one hundred

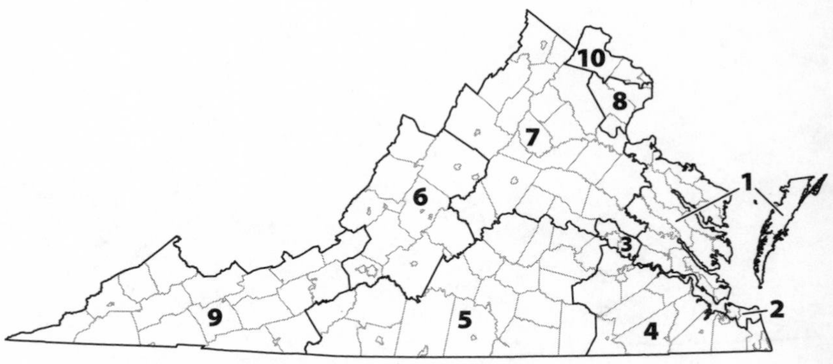

Map 4. Congressional districts created in 1972

members of the House of Delegates, and forty single-member districts for election of senators. The 1971 Senate redistricting law for the first time divided some cities and counties to create single-member districts of roughly equal population in keeping with the principles established in the representation revolution of the 1960s and the directive in the new state constitution. The substantial number of military personnel who resided at the naval base in Norfolk complicated the apportionment of the Senate. The General Assembly adhered to military guidelines and census bureau criteria and counted all naval and military personnel stationed—"homeported"—at the Norfolk Naval Base as residents of the census enumeration district that included the base, even though perhaps as many as half of those people were at sea or lived with their families in civilian residences outside the enumeration district or elsewhere in the region.[15] The General Assembly created three single-member districts that together included all of the city of Norfolk and a portion of the adjacent city of Virginia Beach. The federal court for the Eastern District of Virginia ruled in 1971 in *Howell v. Mahan* that the General Assembly had improperly counted naval personnel as resident in one of the three Norfolk-area districts and ordered that the three districts be combined into one district with three senators to be elected at large.[16] The following year in *Mahan v. Howell* the Supreme Court of the United States affirmed that order.[17]

The federal court for the Eastern District of Virginia, at the same time it ordered the Norfolk Senate districts combined, overturned the law that redistricted the House of Delegates on the basis that its 16.4 percent variation between the least- and most-populous districts was much too great. The judges imposed a redistricting plan on the state that retained the same number of districts, including multimember and floter districts, but in several instances added census enumeration districts in some counties to districts in other counties, subdividing the counties that lost some population to a neighboring legislative district. The judges refused to overturn one innovation in that law, which had divided Fairfax County into two districts with five delegates to be elected at large in each. The court's redistricting altered the boundaries of twenty-eight of the fifty-two districts to reduce the range of variation between least- and most-populous districts to 7.2 percent. The court excepted from that calculation the house district comprised of the Eastern Shore counties of Northampton and Accomack. It contained 6.5 percent fewer people than it should have (and if included in the other calculations would have raised the overall variation to 10.3 percent) because of the "natural isolation" of the two counties, which were not contiguous with any other Virginia counties.[18] The 1971 general election of members of the House of Delegates was the first in which any legislative districts bisected any city or county boundary.

On February 21, 1973, in *Mahan v. Howell* the Supreme Court by a 5 to 3 majority (Virginian Lewis F. Powell took no part in the decision) overturned the district court's invalidation and redistricting of House of Delegates districts in part because the state's traditional reliance on county and city boundaries was a "rational" method to preserve legitimate governmental interests. "We hold," Associate Justice William Rehnquist explained for the majority, "that the legislature's plan for apportionment of the House of Delegates may reasonably be said to advance the rational state policy of respecting the boundaries of political subdivisions," although he remarked that the 16.4 percent variation in population "may well approach tolerable limits."[19] The three dissenting judges believed that the state's arguments in favor of the constitutionality of the law failed to make a persuasive case that the rational goal of adhering to county and city boundaries was actually essential for any stated legitimate public purpose and therefore could not justify the wide variation in population among the districts.[20] The biennial elections of members of the House of Delegates from 1973 through

1979 therefore occurred under authority and with the district lines the General Assembly adopted in 1971, which divided Fairfax County into two multimember districts but required that all other district lines follow traditional county and city boundaries.

At the same time the cities of Petersburg and Richmond were engaged in litigation under the Voting Rights Act.[21] In 1971, following Virginia law that allowed a city to annex adjacent county land through a judicial process,[22] Petersburg annexed fourteen square miles of suburban portions of Prince George and Dinwiddie Counties. That increased the tax base of the city and enlarged its population from 36,103 to 43,426. Most of the new residents were white, which transformed the city from being 55 percent to 46 percent African American. The annexation also provided for enlarging the city council from five to seven members, all elected at large. As section 5 of the Voting Rights Act required, the city submitted its annexation plan to the Department of Justice for approval or rejection. The department ruled that the effect of the annexation was to dilute black voting strength in the city, which had a history of racially polarized voting, even though the two African American members of the city council had voted for the annexation. The city then sued the Justice Department. On March 5, 1973, in *Petersburg v. United States,* the United States District Court for the District of Columbia found no racial motivation for the annexation, but the judges required, as the attorney general had suggested, that city council members be elected from single-member districts rather than at large. Some districts would have black majorities in keeping with the pattern of residential racial segregation, and the city council would probably have a white majority, but single-member council districts would not dilute "the weight, strength and power of the votes of the black voters in the City" as would at-large districts.[23]

The litigation involving the city of Richmond began before the Petersburg annexation and continued after the Petersburg case was concluded. In 1969 Richmond annexed approximately twenty-three square miles of suburban Chesterfield County. Most of the population of the annexed area was white, which transformed the city from being 52 percent African American to 42 percent. As in Petersburg, Richmond's city council had consisted of members elected at-large, nine members in the case of Richmond. On reviewing the annexation as section 5 of the Voting Rights Act required, the U.S. attorney general noted that it "inevitably tends to dilute the voting strength of black voters." He suggested that if the city changed from at-large to single-member districts for the election of council members the annexation would not violate the act.[24]

Several people filed lawsuits to have the annexation declared illegal on any of several grounds. Richmond civil rights activist Curtis Holt filed two. The federal court for the Eastern District of Virginia discovered convincing evidence that some city council members acted from racial motivations to preserve a white voting majority and ordered that voters within the original boundaries elect seven council members at large and voters in the annexed area elect two at large. In *Holt v. City of Richmond* the district court ruled the annexation illegal.[25] The Fourth Circuit Court of Appeals overturned the district court in *City of Richmond v. Holt* on the grounds that the annexation deprived no person of the vote on account of race.[26]

The Supreme Court of the United States agreed to hear all the cases that arose as a result of the annexation. In *City of Richmond v. United States* by a 5 to 3 majority (Powell again taking no part), the badly divided Supreme Court ruled on June 24, 1975, that if the city switched from at-large election of council members to single-member districts the right of no voter would be denied or diluted and that the annexation could stand. The court also confirmed the district court ruling in *Petersburg v. United States* when it applied the same remedy. As a result of the protracted lawsuits and negotiations between the Department of Justice and the city, residents of Richmond were unable to vote for city council members between 1970 and 1977. During that long interval council members first elected in 1970 remained in office.[27]

The Voting Rights Act and the requirements for undiluted African American voting for municipal government councils brought about numerous important changes in local government. One of the most important and conspicuous was that during the 1970s and 1980s many Virginia communities shifted from at-large to district elections for city and town councils and other elective bodies.[28]

The 1981 redistricting of the two houses of the General Assembly resembled a slow-motion train wreck both at the time and in retrospect. To begin with, the census bureau was late in providing 1980 census data to the legislature, which meant that members of the assembly could scarcely begin work until the regularly scheduled session was almost completed and the deadline for candidates to file papers for party primaries was near at hand. Moreover, even though members of the assembly received expert legal advice about the changed legal requirements as well as detailed information about changing population patterns, they ignored it all and proceeded hastily with firm self-confidence and willful ignorance of or indifference to the requirements of the representation revolution of the 1960s.

At a special session of the General Assembly in April 1981, the Senate and House of Delegates each adopted a plan for redistricting its chamber, the other chamber accepted it, and the governor signed them. In July 1981 the Department of Justice refused to approve the redistricting law for the Senate, which provided for forty single-member districts but ran the boundary line between two single-member districts in Norfolk squarely through the area of the city with the largest population of African Americans. State Senator L. Douglas Wilder had unsuccessfully tried to have the district lines drawn differently to preserve the existing black-majority district. In a special session in November the General Assembly adopted a new law for redistricting the Senate, which the department accepted.[29]

For the election of one hundred delegates the April 1981 House of Delegates act created twenty-one single-member districts and thirty-one multimember districts.[30] The law relied heavily on multimember urban and suburban districts and immediately came under criticism as diluting the voting strength of African Americans. The difference between the least- and most-populous districts of the House of Delegates was 26.6 percent. That far exceeded population variations in legislative districts federal courts had already declared unconstitutional. In July the Department of Justice declined to approve the law because it had broken up a black-majority district that contained the city of Emporia and the black majority counties of Greensville, Sussex, Surry, and Charles City and also New Kent (the only county with a white majority) and placed each of the black-majority counties into a different district with white-majority counties so that none of the districts had a black majority. The law also combined Petersburg with predominately white Colonial Heights to create a white-majority district. On August 11, in a second special session the General Assembly adopted a new house plan that created two new black-majority districts, which the Department of Justice approved, even though it still had large population variances and even more multimember and floter districts and fewer single-member districts than the April act. The department's approval was based solely on the consequences of the new districts for minority voting under the Voting Rights Act and was totally unrelated to Fourteenth Amendment one person, one vote requirements.[31]

Several people filed lawsuits to challenge the August 1981 redistricting act for the House of Delegates, some of them on the basis of racial discrimination, some that population variations among the districts remained too great. On August 25, a three-judge panel of the federal court for the Eastern District of Virginia ruled in the combined cases *Cosner v. Dalton* that "tested by every measure, the August 11 Act departs to a much greater degree than the 1971 Act from the goal of fashioning legislative districts of substantially equal population." The judges ascertained that the assembly could have easily reduced the variance between the least- and most-populous districts by drawing lines differently and that the abundance of multimember districts tended to reduce the voting influence of minority groups. Because it was too late for either the assembly or the judges to devise a new apportionment plan for the House of Delegates before the November election, the judges required that members of the House of Delegates to be elected then under the old 1971 apportionment act serve one-year terms rather than two-year terms and that the General Assembly in the meantime adopt a constitutional plan.[32]

At the special session of assembly in November when the legislators passed the second Senate redistricting law, they passed a third bill to redistrict the House of Delegates. The revised house plan increased the number of multimember districts. The legislators' insistence on not subdividing cities or counties made their task almost impossible. Indeed, I vividly remember sitting down early in 1981 with city and county population data, a large sheaf of paper, and a hand calculator and quickly perceiving that without numerous large multimember districts and some floter districts it was impossible to draw house lines that did not vary substantially in population. The only solution I could perceive was to abandon political jurisdiction boundaries as a primary criterion. Governor John Nichols Dalton came to the same conclusion late in the year and vetoed the November redistricting bill because it failed to meet constitutional requirements. "It is my belief," he informed the assembly, "this can best be achieved through single-member districts."[33]

In January 1982 the General Assembly adopted yet another House of Delegates redistricting law that created single-member districts everywhere, including in populous counties, cities, and suburbs, with the exception of the city of Norfolk.[34] The Department of Justice objected to the law because it submerged black voters in Norfolk in one district, it concentrated too much of the black population in a Newport News district, and it divided black population concentrations in Portsmouth and Hampton.[35] Those district configurations in effect reduced the number of districts in which African Americans voters formed majorities or politically potent minorities.

After conferences between legislative leaders and Department of Justice officials the General Assembly finally completed the required redistricting of the House of Delegates in yet another special session with a law in April 1982 that for the first time created one hundred single-member districts without any evident discrimination against African Americans. The law divided all the large cities and most-populous counties into separate single-member districts.[36] That permanently terminated the use of county and city boundary lines that began in 1619 as the primary criterion for legislative districting.

11

PARTISAN REDISTRICTING

The redistricting of legislative and congressional seats for Virginia following the 1990 census produced three lawsuits. None revolved around equality of representation, as if legislators had learned their lessons after 1981 and 1982. One suit directly challenged the partisan motives of the Democratic Party majority in the General Assembly; one focused on whether two Senate districts were compact according to the requirement of the state constitution; and one involved race and therefore also partisanship because political changes in the United States during the twentieth century and the civil rights movement had drawn most African Americans away from their nineteenth-century allegiance to the Republican Party and into the Democratic Party.

Partisanship was on full display during the 1991 session of the General Assembly, which Norfolk State University political scientist Winnett W. Hagens recognized at the time and other commentators fully documented later.[1] Nobody knew then that this was to be the last redistricting session in which the Democratic Party held large majorities in both houses of the General Assembly. Republicans had begun to make gains in the assembly, in part because of the introduction of single-member districts in 1982. Although still holding only thirty-nine of one hundred seats in the House of Delegates and ten of forty in the Senate, Republicans were gaining and threatened more competition for

Democratic Party dominance than at any time since the Readjusters in the 1870s and 1880s.

In redrawing districts for the House of Delegates, the Democratic Party majority passed and Governor L. Douglas Wilder signed a law that placed several Republican delegates in districts with other Republican incumbents.[2] The Republican Party and the Republican legislators filed suit in the federal court for the Western District of Virginia. A three-judge panel acknowledged in *Republican Party of Virginia v. Wilder* on September 10, 1991, that under certain limited circumstances (relying on the Supreme Court's 1986 ruling in *Davis v. Bandemer*)[3] a federal court could entertain a case on the basis that partisan gerrymandering violated the equal protection clause of the Fourteenth Amendment. The judges then ruled that the Republicans had failed to demonstrate two essential preconditions: that the Democrats' law irreparably harmed them; and that Democrats had enacted it solely for partisan purposes. The court dismissed the case.[4]

In November 6, 1992, in *Jamerson v. Womack,* the Supreme Court of Virginia upheld the Senate redistricting act, which had been challenged as a violation of Article II, section 6 in the Constitution of 1970, which required that all legislative districts contain equal populations as nearly as "practicable," and consist of compact and contiguous territory. The 1991 Senate redistricting law, in part at the insistence of Wilder, created a third black-majority Senate district in addition to the two that then existed. To do so, the law formed two large districts in the portion of Virginia south of the James River. The region was comparatively lightly populated and therefore required geographically large districts. The Fifteenth District was 145 miles from east to west, the Eighteenth District 165 miles from east to west.[5] Map 5 clearly shows how long and in places narrow Senate Districts Fifteen and Eighteen were. The court ruled that taking into account all the sometimes competing requirements of representation—equal population, contiguous

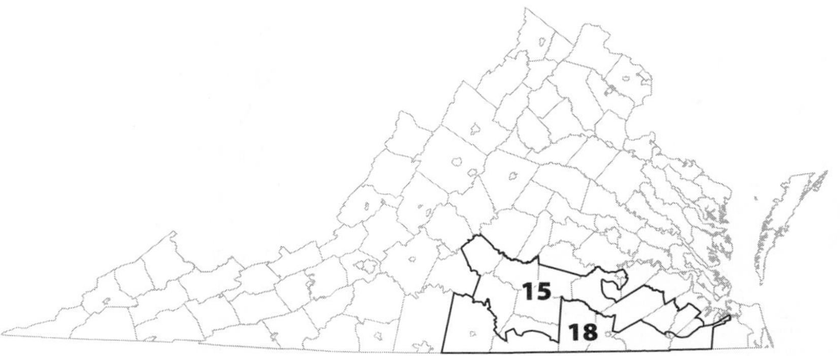

Map 5. State Senate districts created in 1991

territory, compact form, and no devaluation of minority voting strength—the districts were therefore not prima facie unconstitutional and could stand. "The territories of Districts 15 and 18," the judges concluded in a huge understatement, "are not ideal in terms of compactness. Nevertheless, we must give proper deference to the wide discretion accorded the General Assembly in its value judgment of the relative degree of compactness required when reconciling the multiple concerns of apportionment."[6]

The 1991 congressional redistricting act provided for a black-majority district after the 1990 census allowed Virginia an eleventh member of the House of Representatives. Wilder also used his influence with the General Assembly to assure that the newly drawn Third District included a significant black majority to ensure that an African American Democrat would almost certainly be elected.[7] Map 6 shows the House of Representatives districts as adopted in 1991. In 1997, almost six years after passage of the redistricting law, a three-judge panel of the federal court for the Eastern District of Virginia declared in *Moon v. Meadows* that even though the Department of Justice had approved the law, the district violated the Constitution of the United States because the issue of race had played a controlling part in how the

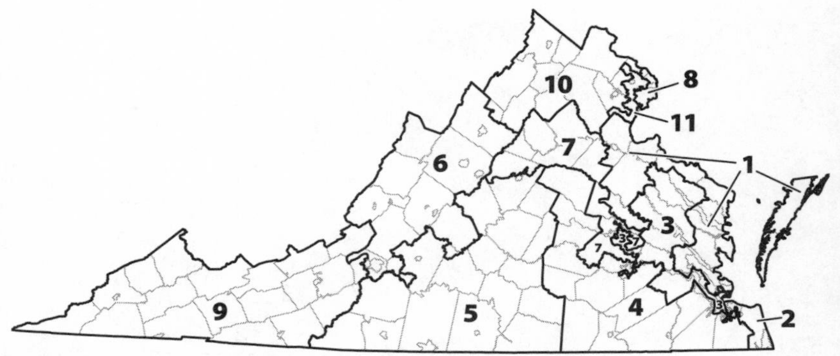

Map 6. Congressional districts created in 1991

"racially-gerrymandered" district had been designed. The court repeatedly criticized the district's "bizarre geographical boundaries" and its "unwieldy and distended shape" that provided an apparently safe congressional seat for an African American candidate.[8]

The 1998 law the General Assembly passed to reconfigure the district (and as a consequence some of the adjacent districts)[9] stood with some changes in 2001 and 2011[10] until challenged as a racial gerrymander again in 2014. In that year in *Page v. Virginia State Board of Elections* and again in 2015 in a second case of the same name, the federal court for the Eastern District of Virginia declared it a violation of the equal protection clause as a racial gerrymander.[11] In 2016, following the failure of the General Assembly to amend the law, the court in *Personhuballah v. Alcorn* drew new district lines.[12]

The 2001 acts that drew new districts for Virginia's congressional delegation and both houses of the General Assembly were the first Republicans shaped. Having replaced the Democratic Party as the majority party in the General Assembly in the 1999 general elections, Republicans finally had and used the opportunity to redraw legislative district boundaries to enlarge and protect their majorities, just as Democrats had formerly done.[13] *Richmond Times-Dispatch* political analyst Jeff E. Schapiro has called the twenty-first-century legislative redistricting acts "hyperpartisan gerrymandering."[14]

In November 2002 in *Wilkins v. West* the Supreme Court of Virginia ruled against challenges to fifteen of the one hundred House of Delegates districts and six of the forty Senate districts on the grounds that they were insufficiently compact or contiguous and also largely or entirely based on race, although the court admitted in some instances "there is a high correlation between race and political affiliation."[15] Two years later the Fourth Circuit Court of Appeals in *Hall v. Virginia* rejected a challenge to the congressional reapportionment act on the grounds that it illegally diluted African American voting strength in the Fourth Congressional District by shifting some precincts from the Fourth to the Third Congressional District.[16] By then the state's congressional districts could by no reasonable criteria be defined as meeting the requirement of the state constitution that they be compact in shape. Among the several criteria for redistricting, legislators and judges have almost always sacrificed compactness to protect any or all of the others.

The redistricting of the two houses of the General Assembly after the 2010 census allowed the Republicans, who had a large majority in the House of Delegates, to create even more safe districts for members of their party.[17] Sophisticated computer technology developed during the previous quarter of a century enabled partisans to analyze population data and voting behavior down to and even below voting district levels and devise redistricting laws that created districts of substantially equal population, which, even though they were obviously drawn for partisan advantage, met all the criteria of the one person, one vote judicial precedents and passed muster under the reviews the Voting Acts Right required.[18] At that time students at nine Virginia universities, some of them law students, used the same information and technologies legislators and their consultants employed to prepare redistricting plans not based on partisan motivation. Their work highlighted the partisanship of the Republican majorities in the General Assembly.[19]

The 2011 law that redistricted the House of Delegates faced challenges in both state and federal courts, but the issues the cases raised did not explicitly target partisan motivation or consequence. Several people challenged the redistricting act on the grounds that it violated the stipulation in Article II, section 6 of the Constitution of 1970 that legislative districts be compact in shape. Their objective was to make partisan gerrymandering more difficult. The Supreme Court of Virginia ruled in *Vesilind v. Virginia State Board of Elections et al.* on May 31, 2018, that even though many of the districts were of odd shapes and differing sizes, the court had no recognized standards by which to ascertain whether districts met the mandate of the state's constitution that districts be compact. None of the more than twenty available and in some instances complex mathematical models for measuring degrees of compactness had received judicial or legislative sanction. When experts applied some of them to the Virginia districts they produced varying results. Lacking an uncontested, reliable method for measuring compactness, the justices of the Supreme Court unanimously refrained from declaring that the redistricting act violated the requirement of the Virginia constitution.[20]

The justices could have been bolder and gone further to declare that at least some of the districts were prima facie not compact without citing any authorities to justify the conclusion. Their predecessors had done just that in *Brown v. Saunders* in 1932 when they invalidated the congressional redistricting act of that year because the districts were not even close to the constitutionally required equal populations. There, mere statement of the variation of numbers in the districts had then been ample proof.[21] A declaration that some of the districts were prima facie violations of the requirement for compactness would have forced the issue of how to devise an acceptable means of measuring compactness, much as the long series of 1960s court decisions had led to the development of uniform national standards for meeting the various one person, one vote criteria.[22]

A three-judge panel of the federal court for the Eastern District of Virginia ruled on challenges to twelve of the one hundred 2011 House of Delegates districts on the basis that they were racial gerrymanders. Legislatures and courts have had to grapple with conflicting requirements that push and pull in opposite directions. The Fourteenth Amendment and section 5 of the Voting Rights Act then required that race not be the dominant factor in redistricting; but section 2 of the Voting Rights Act as amended also required then that changes to voting laws and electoral districts not diminish or dilute the electoral influence of certain designated minorities, usually African Americans.[23] In *Bethune-Hill v. Virginia State Board of Elections* in 2015 the federal court found that one district was an illegal racial gerrymander according to federal legal precedents but that the other eleven were not. Each district had an African American majority in 2010, but almost all had fewer residents than the required 1 percent of the state's population. The General Assembly added voting districts from neighboring jurisdictions to those legislative districts and did so following a rule of thumb that approximately 55 percent of the voting age population of each district be African American. Delegates who designed the districts included both Republican Party leaders and incumbents in those districts, most of whom were African American Democrats. They agreed on that strategy in order not to reduce African American representation in the House of Delegates and thereby appear to violate section 2 of the Voting Rights Act. Testimony at two trials in the federal court for the Eastern District of Virginia fully proved that fact.[24]

The judges' rationale for that decision was the requirement in section 2 of the Voting Rights Acts as amended to 2011 that prevented states from changing electoral districts or voting laws in a manner that reduced the reasonable probability that a designated racial minority could continue to elect members of the legislature—that white legislators could not legislate black legislators out of office. An assumption that African Americans were less likely to vote than white Virginians may have suggested the propriety of requiring a 55 percent majority of voting age African Americans in the districts. The two federal judges who voted for the majority opinion believed that was an acceptable method of conforming Virginia's election districts to the requirements of the Voting Rights Act, even though legislators evidently arrived at the 55 percent proportion informally and without any legal precedent or government-established criteria. The judges ascertained that for eleven districts, traditional criteria (protecting incumbents, following city, county, or voting district lines or waterways) justified the resulting district boundaries. Race, the judges concluded, did not predominate over traditional redistricting criteria, so the districts were not therefore illegal racial gerrymanders.[25]

The plaintiffs appealed the decision to the Supreme Court of the United States. On March 1, 2017, in *Bethune-Hill v. Virginia State Board of Elections* the court unanimously ruled (with one justice dissenting from part of the reasoning) that the prominence of race embodied in the arbitrary 55 percent criterion should have required the district court to apply a stricter rule of scrutiny. The Supreme Court sent the case back to the district court with instructions to apply the stricter rules the Supreme Court had specified in *Alabama Legislative Black Caucus v. Alabama* in 2015,[26] the same year in which the district court in Virginia issued its decision. That rule required that if race is taken into account in redistricting, race could not even be a major factor, and certainly not the predominating factor.[27]

The federal court for the Eastern District of Virginia declared in its second ruling in *Bethune-Hill v. Virginia State Board of*

Elections on June 26, 2018, in a two-to-one opinion (written by the judge who dissented in 2015) that all twelve districts were illegal racial gerrymanders based in large part on the arbitrary 55 percent rule. The court gave the General Assembly a deadline of October 30, 2018, to pass a constitutionally acceptable revision of the 2011 redistricting law for use in the 2019 legislative elections.[28] The governor called a special redistricting session of the General Assembly, which met for one day on August 30, 2018. Democrats introduced a redistricting bill, but Republicans failed to present a plan and merely criticized the Democratic bill as partisan. Republicans appealed to the Supreme Court to overturn the federal district court or postpone the October 30 deadline.[29] Two weeks after the deadline the Supreme Court of the United States agreed to hear the Republicans' appeal.[30] Meantime, the assembly reconvened on September 27. At that time a Republican majority in committee killed the Democratic bill, and the governor promised to veto the proposed Republican bill if it passed.[31] Then on October 5 the Republican Speaker of the House of Delegates informed the federal court that the assembly would not again meet before the redistricting deadline.[32] Therefore, on February 14, 2019, the district court issued an order that reconfigured all the districts and made minor adjustments to several adjacent districts. Those will be the electoral districts for the 2019 general election because on June 17, the Supreme Court rejected the challenge Republicans in the House of Delegates filed and let the district court's redistricting order stand.[33]

The original 2011 law had increased Republican strength in the House of Delegates in part because of the transfer of African Americans from politically competitive districts or districts with white or Republican majorities into districts with black majorities to bring the latter up to the 55 percent level. While that made some Democratic incumbents politically safe, it also made adjoining districts whiter, and in some instances it converted those districts from politically competitive to relatively safer for Republicans. In the 1990s Hagens had correctly predicted that single-member districts and reapportionment that favored election of more African Americans would at the same time favor the election of more Republicans.[34]

That method of shifting voters of one party (African Americans usually voted Democratic in twenty-first-century Virginia) into districts with other people of the same party is a partisan gerrymandering technique called packing. It virtually assured in this instance that a certain number of African American Democrats would win election to the House of Delegates, but at the same time it increased the chances that a larger number of white Republicans would win election in other districts. With or without racial motivations, packing is a popular method of gerrymandering for partisan purposes. So is its opposite, called cracking, in which clusters of voters with a history of voting for one party are broken up and distributed among other districts in which their party forms a minority. That can also produce an increased number of victories for the other party. The party in control of a legislature during a redistricting session and intent on partisan gerrymandering chooses packing or cracking depending in part on how evenly members of the other party are distributed across the landscape. In Virginia, especially in urban and suburban areas, the long-lasting legacy of enforced residential racial segregation has produced large regions that easily lend themselves to packing. That was one of the political consequences of the 2011 redistricting of the House of Delegates, even though the federal court in its 2018 decision did not seriously consider partisan motivations or consequences.

The crucial 2019 legislative elections will be conducted under different conditions and with some different House of Delegates districts than those adopted in 2011 and therefore with unpredictable consequences for members of the two political parties. The short- and long-term political consequences of *Bethune-Hill v.*

Virginia State Board of Elections and the subsequent U.S. Supreme Court case, *Virginia House of Delegates et al. v. Bethune-Hill et al.*, may benefit Democratic legislators and candidates at the expense of Republicans. That could continue some recent electoral trends. Since the 2001 redistricting of Virginia's congressional and legislative seats the behavior of the voters in statewide elections (Democrats and Republicans are very unevenly distributed across the landscape) demonstrates that Democrats and Republicans are fairly evenly matched, with evidence of a slight advantage for Democrats that may be slowly increasing.[35] Democrats won three of four elections for president (75 percent), five of six elections for United States senator (83.3 percent), four of five elections for governor (80 percent), three of five elections for lieutenant governor (60 percent), and two of five elections for attorney general (40 percent). The forty-member Virginia Senate has remained almost equally divided for the entire time with never more than a three-vote majority for either party. In 160 general elections for members of the Senate, Democrats won 78 (49 percent). Partisan gerrymandering, though, has been clearly evident in races for the House of Representatives and the House of Delegates. Partisan districting contributed to Democrats winning only 34 of 99 general elections to the House of Representatives (34.3 percent) and 341 of 900 general elections for the House of Delegates (38 percent)—if counting independent delegate Lacey Putney as a Democrat; he caucused with the Democratic delegates for much of that time but often voted with the Republicans. That pattern is almost exactly the reverse of the pattern from the 1970s through the mid-1990s when under partisan Democratic redistricting Republican candidates won all presidential elections in the state, five of eight gubernatorial elections, and elected significant numbers of congressmen and United States senators, but at the same time Democrats regularly won large majorities in both houses of the General Assembly.

And at the same time, during the early years of the twenty-first century legislators in several states, including in Virginia, have imposed new restrictions and requirements on the processes of registration and voting on the pretext of preventing electoral fraud. None of the legislatures has adduced the existence of any serious voting irregularities, however, which has led some informed observers to describe the new laws as solutions in search of a problem. Some Republican sponsors of those laws, though, have been openly clear that their purpose was to reduce the number of Democratic voters. Those legislators evidently believed that Latinos, African Americans, and perhaps some other ethnic minorities who might have more difficulty meeting the new requirements were likely to vote Democratic.[36] These laws recall the poll tax, difficult registration tests, and literacy requirements of an earlier era, designed to disfranchise African American voters.

12

THE POLITICAL AND LEGAL LANDSCAPES IN VIRGINIA IN 2019

In the reapportionment of the House of Representatives after the 2020 census, Virginia may possibly gain a twelfth congressional seat, and the nationwide redistricting of congressional and legislative districts will begin in 2021. People who are anticipating those events may feel as if they are standing on a frozen river during a spring warm spell. The political and legal contexts, like the ice in such a river, could be unpredictably shifting under their feet. Nobody knows whether the ice, the politics, or the law will break up, shift into a new configuration, or remain frozen.

In the November 2017 elections Virginia voters reduced the two-thirds Republican majority in the House of Delegates to a mere two votes. Because of the partisan gerrymandering in 2011, the result was a great surprise. Whether the particular circumstances of the 2017 election dissipate before the 2019 election and allow Republicans to regain some or most of their almost veto-proof majority or whether the partial 2019 redistricting of the House of Delegates will further reduce their strength remains to be seen. The 2019 election could have very important and long-lasting consequences because the legislators elected in 2019 will redistrict both houses of the General Assembly and the state's congressional districts in 2021 if voters do not ratify a proposed constitutional amendment to create a bipartisan redistricting commission.

The political context in Virginia appears to make hyperpartisan gerrymandering less likely than at any legislative session in more than half a century. In fact, the circumstance in 2021 could be unprecedented. It could be the first redistricting session in which neither party has a dominant role in either or both houses of the assembly. If in 2021 the partisan alignment in both houses is fairly close, and if Republicans anticipate that a Democratic governor would veto a very partisan redistricting bill, that could force members of both parties to move toward a less-partisan redistricting. If one party has a substantial majority in one house and the other party has a substantial majority in the other, the politics of redistricting could become much more complicated, perhaps more partisan rather than less.

The legal landscape has changed, too, and might or might not change more. In *Shelby County v. Holder* in 2013 the Supreme Court of the United States declared that section 4(b) of the Voting Rights Act of 1965 as amended several times violated the Constitution of the United States on the disputed basis that its most recent revision relied on outdated and therefore constitutionally unacceptable criteria when it singled out for special oversight states and parts of states that had histories of racially discriminatory voting laws and practices.[1] The court did not invalidate section 5 of the act, which required those states to submit election laws or laws that altered jurisdictional boundaries or electoral districts to the Department of Justice or to the federal court for the District of Columbia for approval; but without the provisions of section 4(b) that enumerated those jurisdictions, section 5 could no longer require them to apply for preclearance of changed voting laws. Any laws states pass will be in effect unless and until successfully challenged in court.

Even without the preclearance obligation of the Voting Rights Act, the large body of judicial precedent beginning with the representation revolution of the 1960s has required that redistricting not discriminate against any group of people because of race, occupation, place of residence, or any other factor not demonstrably designed to enable a state to achieve some specific legitimate governmental objective. Those decisions defined some of the principles that people have used to question the constitutionality of partisan gerrymanders. High on their list of criteria is a right to free association, which federal courts have long ruled lies within the free speech clause of the First Amendment—that people may associate and act together for political purposes without governmental hindrance or discrimination. Precedents do not clearly indicate how a challenge to partisan gerrymandering on the grounds that it denied or diluted the right of association would fare, either at the district court or appellate court level.[2]

Since the federal courts entered the political thicket in 1962 judges have occasionally hinted that partisan districting could be within their jurisdiction, but the Supreme Court has never decided a redistricting case in which the constitutionality of partisan gerrymanders was the sole consideration. The justices always settled cases in which partisan districting was raised on some narrower ground such as a jurisdictional or procedural question, without creating new precedent or deciding how much partisanship is too much or how to measure it. In practice, devising criteria for that purpose has been extremely difficult.[3] The situation early in the twenty-first century with respect to partisan gerrymandering is in some respects analogous to that early in the 1960s when legislators and courts had not yet established clear criteria for ascertaining how much deviation from the perfect one person, one vote equality was too much.

In 2016 Michael Parsons published a detailed review in the *William and Mary Bill of Rights Journal* of how federal judges and members of the Supreme Court have commented on partisan gerrymandering. He suggested that the members of the Supreme Court have ample and adequate precedent and could very well decide that federal courts should take the unprecedented step of ruling on the constitutionality of partisan gerrymandering, the thorniest part of the political thicket.[4] If so, the constitutional and legal requirements for redistricting at all levels could change yet again, as they did during the 1960s. If they do, it will be another instance in which people's ideas about representative government undermined or overturned long-established political practices and legal precedents. But the obstacles to any lawsuit that challenges redistricting on the sole basis of partisanship remain numerous and high.

In 2018 the Supreme Court of the United States declined to rule on the substance of three partisan redistricting cases. The lead case was *Gill v. Whitford,* on appeal from the federal court for the Western District of Wisconsin. There, in November 2016 the federal court in *Whitford v. Gill* invalidated a law for redistricting the state legislature on the grounds that it was excessively partisan in intent and effect,[5] the first such major federal court ruling of its kind. On June 18, 2018, the Supreme Court unanimously declared that the several people who challenged the redistricting law did not have standing to sue in order to invalidate the entire redistricting law. Relying on numerous precedents, the justices explained that the individual citizens could sue only to invalidate the boundaries of the particular district in which each of them resided, because it would be the configuration of that district alone that might deny or damage any of them in the exercise of a constitutionally guaranteed right. The portions of the redistricting law that applied to other parts of the state did not individually injure them, so therefore they consequently did not have standing to sue to invalidate the entire law. The court remanded the case to the district court for further action.[6]

All nine members of the Supreme Court joined in the ruling, but the directive to remand the case to the district court was not unanimous. Two justices filed an opinion concurring in the ruling but dissenting from the order to remand the case on the grounds that precedents that defined standing should have led the Supreme Court to dismiss the case. That would have left the redistricting law in effect. Four other justices filed a separate concurring opinion that suggested means by which the case could be reshaped so as to avoid the issue of standing and bring the substantive issue of partisan gerrymandering back before the Supreme Court. That was highly unusual. In effect, seven of nine justices appeared willing to have the legal issue of partisan gerrymandering adjudicated in federal court. Justice Anthony Kennedy, who voted to remand the case but was not one of the four justices who joined in the concurring opinion, announced his retirement a few days later. That retirement and replacement by a new justice may make it even more difficult to predict whether the Supreme Court would be willing to rule on the issue of partisan redistricting if—more likely, when—the Wisconsin case or a similar case comes back to the Supreme Court in a different guise.

On the same day the Supreme Court issued its ruling in *Gill v. Whitford* it unanimously refused in *Benisek v. Lamone* to intervene in a case in the federal district court in Maryland that challenged the Maryland legislature's redrawing of a congressional district line to convert a safe Republican district into a Democratic district.[7] And one week later the justices unanimously vacated the January 2018 decision of the federal court for the Middle District of North Carolina in *Common Cause et al. v. Rucho.* That court had invalidated that state's congressional redistricting law on the grounds that it was excessively partisan in intent and effect.[8] In an unsigned order without dissent or written opinion the Supreme Court remanded the case to the district court for further consideration based on the ruling in *Gill v. Whitford.* Together, the three rulings suggest that members of the Supreme Court may not in fact be willing to confront the issue of partisan gerrymandering. Because all three decisions focused on whether plaintiffs had standing to sue, the rulings did not clearly address partisan redistricting as a constitutional issue.

The justices, did, however, discuss in *Gill v. Whitford* other barriers that people who challenge partisan gerrymanders faced. How could a partisan redistricting deprive a voter of a constitutionally protected right in a district within a region in which the voter's party formed a small minority or a large majority? Adjustments to district lines might not change anything of consequence for that voter, and the one person, one vote requirement of the equal protection clause of the Fourteenth Amendment does not guarantee that voters have the right to elect their preferred candidates to office. Adjustments of electoral district lines in a region with a history of nearly always voting for one party might not significantly alter predictable outcomes in the districts that comprise the region. Would a voter in such a district have standing to sue? The justices alluded to this in taking into account arguments of counsel. Should courts take such circumstances into account in assessing partisanship and whether such schemes damage or deny any voter in the exercise of a constitutionally protected right? What are the implications for standing? How can courts define or measure an allegedly partisan consequence? How much might be too much? What constitutionally protected right or rights would be damaged or endangered? Could a lawsuit for the purpose of invalidating a partisan gerrymander be brought as a class action suit (on behalf of the named plaintiffs and all other persons similarly circumstanced) that avoided the question of standing? What remedies could courts apply?

A challenge to partisan redistricting succeeded in the Supreme Court of Pennsylvania in 2018. In *League of Women Voters et al. v. Pennsylvania* the court declared that the state's congressional districting law violated the state's constitution as excessively partisan in intent and effect. The judges based their decision entirely on the language of Article I, section 5 of the Pennsylvania Constitution of 1968, which requires that "Elections shall be free and equal." The judges traced that language back to the Pennsylvania Constitution of 1776, which had required that "all elections ought to be free; and that all free men having a sufficient evident common interest with, and attachment to the community, have a right to elect officers." Article II, section 16 of the Pennsylvania Constitution of 1968 also requires that "representative districts . . . shall be composed of compact and contiguous territory as nearly equal in population as practicable."[9]

The free elections provision in the Pennsylvania Constitution of 1776 was clearly adapted (in fact, it was in part copied) from the 1776 Virginia Declaration of Rights that is still a part of Article I, section 6 of the Virginia Constitution of 1970;[10] and the language that requires equal population and compact and contiguous districts is almost indistinguishable from that in the same section of the Virginia Constitution. The Pennsylvanians had made an important change to the free elections provision, though, that was critical in the 2018 court case. To the original Virginia phrase that elections "be free," they added the two words, "and equal," which the Virginia Constitution has never required. The equal protection clause of the Fourteenth Amendment, however, could require that redistricting criteria in the Constitution of Virginia be applied in the same manner as the Supreme Court of Pennsylvania prescribed.

The Pennsylvania decision is not a binding precedent on the Supreme Court of Virginia should it ever be called on to decide whether a congressional or legislative redistricting act is unconstitutional for the sole or primary reason of being partisan or excessively partisan. The decision could, however, be employed as a useful precedent in a federal court to explain the manner in which the language of the Pennsylvania Constitution illuminates the meaning of the very similar language in the Virginia Constitution of 1970. That appears to be unlikely in the short term. Associate

Justice of the Supreme Court of the United States Samuel Alito twice refused to allow an appeal of the Pennsylvania Supreme Court's decision to the federal courts because it dealt exclusively with requirements of the state's constitution and therefore did not involve a federally protected right.[11] The state supreme court redistricted the state's congressional districts after the legislature refused to do so.

The year 2018 was an important but inconclusive one in the jurisprudence of partisan gerrymandering, both in federal and state courts. It was also an important year in the legal scholarship of redistricting, reapportionment, and gerrymandering. The April 2018 issue of the *William and Mary Law Review* published fifteen substantial articles (more than 750 pages in total), derived from a 2017 symposium, "2020 Redistricting: Mapping a New Political Debate," at the Marshall-Wythe School of Law at the College of William and Mary. The articles describe, analyze, and critique the case law, litigation, and legal scholarship on different aspects of the three interrelated topics.

In this changed but uncertain legal environment the General Assembly of Virginia will draw new district lines for the House of Representatives, the House of Delegates, and the state Senate in 2021 unless a proposed amendment to the state constitution is ratified to create a bipartisan redistricting commission. The startling election results of 2017, the 2019 partial redistricting of the House of Delegates, and the unpredictable results of the 2019 election, in which all members of both houses will be up for re-election, may further alter the political context in which the assembly redistricts the state.

The difficulty of ascertaining political intentions and whether too much partisanship is embedded in a redistricting law have made, and may continue to make, adjudication a poor vehicle for solving a widely acknowledged political problem. Changes to state constitutions could offer a better opportunity. The nonpartisan coalition OneVirginia2021, which has as its goal the elimination of partisan districting in the state, created a bipartisan taskforce in August 2018 to propose an amendment to the state constitution to create an independent commission that would redistrict the state, and therefore remove that responsibility from partisan politicians.[12] As of that date four western states—Washington, Idaho, California, and Arizona—had independent commissions for that purpose,[13] and proposals to establish commissions were then pending in several other states.

Late in the 2019 session the General Assembly passed a joint resolution to amend the constitution and create a bipartisan redistricting commission to redistrict both house of the General Assembly and the state's congressional districts. If would consist of two members of each party from each house and eight citizen members that leaders of the two parties in both houses would appoint from a list of sixteen people that a committee of retired judges selected. A supermajority would be required for the commission to adopt a plan, which would mean that some members of both parties would have to approve it. For the Senate and House of Delegates, the commission would prepare one plan for redistricting both houses, rather than separate plans for each as in the past. The assembly would have the option to accept or reject but not amend it.[14] Following the 2019 elections the newly elected legislators would have to pass the joint resolution again in 2020 before it could be submitted to the voters for ratification or rejection in the autumn of 2020, only a few months before the required redistricting in 2021.

NOTES

1. The Gerrymander Monster

1. Elmer C. Griffith, *The Rise and Development of the Gerrymander* (Chicago, 1907), 16–20; Kenneth C. Martis, "The Original Gerrymander," *Political Geography* 27 (2008): 833–39.

2. Griffith, *Rise and Development of the Gerrymander,* 7.

3. Brent Tarter, *The Grandees of Government: The Origins and Persistence of Undemocratic Politics in Virginia* (Charlottesville, Va., 2013).

2. The Colonial Background

1. William J. Van Schreeven and George H. Reese, eds., *Proceedings of the General Assembly of Virginia, July 3–August 4, 1619* (Jamestown, Va., 1969), including on even-numbered pages a facsimile of the original in the National Archives of Great Britain, PRO CO 1/1, and on odd-numbered pages a transcription; for the conditions under which the first assembly met and what it did, see Jon Kukla, *Speakers and Clerks of the Virginia House of Burgesses, 1619–1776* (Richmond, Va., 1981), 3–10, 31–34; Jon Kukla, *Political Institutions in Virginia, 1619–1660* (New York, 1989), 40–64; Warren M. Billings, *A Little Parliament: The Virginia General Assembly in the Seventeenth Century* (Richmond, Va., 2004), 5–10; Brent Tarter, *The Grandees of Government: The Origins and Persistence of Undemocratic Politics in Virginia* (Charlottesville, Va., 2013), 11–32.

2. *Oxford English Dictionary,* s.v. "burgess."

3. Yeardley's instructions are evidently lost, but company officials copied them for Sir Francis Wyatt's use later, for which see Susan Myra Kingsbury, ed., *Records of the Virginia Company of London,* 4 vols. (Washington, D.C., 1906–35), 3:483–84.

4. Wyatt's warrant, Kingsbury, ed., *Records,* 4:449.

5. Kukla, *Political Institutions,* 110–22; Billings, *Little Parliament,* 27–28.

6. William Waller Hening, ed., *The Statutes at Large: Being a Collection of All the Laws of Virginia, from the First Session of the Legislature, in the Year 1619 . . . ,* 13 vols. (Richmond, Va., etc., 1809–23), 1:299–300.

7. Hening, *Statutes at Large,* 2:20, 272–73.

8. Hening, *Statutes at Large,* 1:421, 520–21; Tarter, *Grandees of Government,* 35–53.

9. Hening, *Statues at Large,* 3:236–46, 4:475–78.

10. Charter of Williamsburg printed in *William and Mary Quarterly,* 1st ser., 10 (1901): 84–91; *Copy of the Charter of Norfolk Borough, Incorporated the 15th September, 1736* (Norfolk, Va., 1797), 2–14, also reprinted in Brent Tarter, ed., *The Order Book and Related Papers of the Common Hall of the Borough of Norfolk, Virginia, 1736–1798* (Richmond, Va., 1979), 35–41.

11. Cynthia Miller Leonard, comp., *The General Assembly of Virginia, July 30, 1619–January 11, 1978: A Bicentennial Register of Members* (Richmond, Va., 1978), 73, 77.

12. Hening, *Statutes at Large,* 2:280.

13. Hening, *Statutes at Large,* 3:26.

14. Hening, *Statutes at Large,* 3:172–75, quotation on 172.

15. Hening, *Statutes at Large,* 4:475–76; Albert Edward McKinley, *The Suffrage Franchise in the Thirteen American Colonies* (Philadelphia, 1903), 40.

16. Northampton Co. Order Book 10 (1664–74): fol. 91. Compilations of colonial statutes did not include the act, which exists only in the one text copied into the county court's records.

17. Susie M. Ames, "The Reunion of Two Virginia Counties," *Journal of Southern History* 4 (1942): 536–48.

3. Representation in Revolutionary Virginia

1. Records of the convention that adopted it are preserved in Revolutionary Convention Papers, Record Group 89, Library of Virginia, and printed in vols. 6–7 of William J. Van Schreeven, Robert L. Scribner, and Brent Tarter, eds., *Revolutionary Virginia, the Road to Independence: A Documentary Record,* 7 vols. (Charlottesville, Va., 1973–83); accounts of the convention are in Edmund Randolph, *History of Virginia,* ed. Arthur H. Shaffer (Charlottesville, 1970), 250–63; Hugh Blair Grigsby, *The Virginia Convention of 1776* (Richmond, Va., 1855); Robert L. Hildrup, "The Virginia Convention of 1776" (PhD diss., University of Virginia, 1935); John E. Selby, *The Revolution in Virginia, 1775–1783* (Williamsburg, Va., 1988), 95–123;

[Brent Tarter], "An Introductory Note," in *Revolutionary Virginia, the Road to Independence,* 7:1–18; and Brent Tarter, *The Grandees of Government: The Origins and Persistence of Undemocratic Politics in Virginia* (Charlottesville, Va., 2013), 114–36. Lacking an authenticated enrolled parchment, the most authentic texts of the Constitution of 1776 and the Declaration of Rights are printed in the convention's official *Ordinances Passed at a Convention of Delegates and Representatives, From the Several Counties and Corporations of Virginia, Held at the Capitol, in the City of Williamsburg, on Monday the 6th of May, Anno Dom: 1776* (Williamsburg, Va., 1776), 3–13. Because the Constitution of 1776 was not divided into articles and sections it is necessary to cite page numbers from the officially printed text for this state constitution rather than the customary citations to articles and sections.

2. *Ordinances Passed at a Convention,* 7–8.

3. For Richmond, William Waller Hening, ed., *The Statutes at Large: Being a Collection of All the Laws of Virginia, from the First Session of the Legislature, in the Year 1619 . . . ,* 13 vols. (Richmond, Va., etc., 1809–23), 12:722–33. For Petersburg, *Acts of Assembly,* 1815–16 sess., chap. 82.

4. Van Schreeven, Scribner, and Tarter, *Revolutionary Virginia, the Road to Independence,* 7:654.

5. Van Schreeven, Scribner, and Tarter, *Revolutionary Virginia, the Road to Independence,* 7:690, 697, 698; Hening, *Statutes at Large,* 9:128–30.

6. J. R. Pole, "Representation and Authority in Virginia from the Revolution to Reform," *Journal of Southern History* 24 (1958): 16–50; J. R. Pole, *Political Representation in England and the Origins of the American Revolution* (London, 1966); Jackson Turner Main, *The Upper House in Revolutionary America, 1763–1788* (Madison, Wis., 1967); Gordon S. Wood, *The Creation of the American Republic, 1776–1787* (Chapel Hill, N.C., 1969), 162–96, 206–26, 237–55; John Phillip Reid, *The Concept of Representation in the Age of the American Revolution* (Chicago, 1989); Peverill Squire, *The Rise of the Representative: Lawmakers and Constituents in Colonial America* (Ann Arbor, Mich., 2017).

7. Hening, *Statutes at Large,* 4:475–78.

8. Tarter, *Grandees of Government,* 121, 131–34.

9. *Ordinances Passed at a Convention,* 4.

10. *Ordinances Passed at a Convention,* 8.

11. Randolph, *History of Virginia,* 256–57.

12. Hening, *Statutes at Large,* 12:120–21.

13. Tarter, *Grandees of Government,* 85–110, in part following Jack P. Greene, "Society, Ideology, and Politics: An Analysis of the Political Culture of Mid-Eighteenth-Century Virginia," in *Society, Freedom and Conscience: The American Revolution in Virginia, Massachusetts, and New York,* ed. Richard M. Jellison (New York, 1976), 14–76; and John G. Kolp, *Gentlemen and Freeholders: Political Practices in Colonial Virginia* (Baltimore, 1998), both of which significantly revise Charles S. Sydnor, *Gentlemen Freeholders: Political Practices in Washington's Virginia* (Chapel Hill, N.C., 1952), 2nd ed., *American Revolutionaries in the Making: Political Practices in Washington's Virginia* (New York, 1965); and Robert E. Brown and B. Katherine Brown, *Virginia, 1705–1786: Democracy or Aristocracy?* (East Lansing, Mich., 1964).

14. "Decius," in *Virginia Independent Chronicle* (Richmond), February 25, 1789 (printed in all italic type), and excerpted in Merrill Jensen et al., eds., *Documentary History of the First Federal Elections, 1788–1790,* 4 vols. (Madison, Wis., 1976–89), 2:392–93.

15. Hening, *Statutes at Large,* 12:653–56.

16. Elmer C. Griffith, *The Rise and Development of the Gerrymander* (Chicago, 1907), 31–42; Thomas Rogers Hunter, "The First Gerrymander? Patrick Henry, James Madison, James Monroe, and Virginia's 1788 Congressional Districting," *Early American Studies* 9 (2011): 781–820; Jon Kukla, *Patrick Henry, Champion of Liberty* (New York, 2017), 352–53.

17. Richard Labunsky, *James Madison and the Struggle for the Bill of Rights* (New York, 2006), 178–240.

18. Tarter, *Grandees of Government,* 132–33.

19. Griffith, *Rise and Development of the Gerrymander,* 46–47, 82–85.

4. A Gerrymander in Fact Though Not in Name

1. Thomas Jefferson, *Notes on the State of Virginia,* ed. William Peden (Chapel Hill, N.C., 1955), 117–20, quotations on 118, 119.

2. Kentucky Constitution of 1792, Art. I.

3. *Alexandria Herald,* June 3, 1816.

4. Proceedings and public declaration printed in *Richmond Enquirer,* August 31, 1816, and *Niles' Weekly Register* 3 (September 14, 1816), 37–40, quotation on 38.

5. William Waller Hening, ed., *The Statutes at Large: Being a Collection of All the Laws of Virginia, from the First Session of the Legislature, in the Year*

1619 . . . , 13 vols. (Richmond, Va., etc., 1809–23), 10:140–45; Brent Tarter, *The Grandees of Government: The Origins and Persistence of Undemocratic Politics in Virginia* (Charlottesville, Va., 2013), 130–31.

6. *Acts of Assembly,* 1816–17 sess., chap. 5; Elmer C. Griffith, *The Rise and Development of the Gerrymander* (Chicago, 1907), 102–03, failed to perceive the full import of the deliberate skewing of representation in favor of the eastern, slave-owning region of the state, perhaps because the law did not appear to benefit a political party or faction, and also because he misconstrued part of the 1817 law and ignored other parts, as well as the purpose and effect of the prior 1782 law.

7. Tarter, *Grandees of Government,* 185–89; on the pervasive importance of slavery in state constitutional and statute law, see Robin L. Einhorn, *American Taxation, American Slavery* (Chicago, 2006).

5. The Great Gerrymander of 1830

1. Records of the convention, including the authenticated enrolled parchment constitution, are preserved in Records of the Virginia Constitutional Convention of 1829–30, Record Group 91, Library of Virginia, and printed in *Journal, Acts and Proceedings of a General Convention of the Commonwealth of Virginia, Assembled in Richmond* (Richmond, Va., 1829 [i.e., 1830]), which includes the texts of the Declaration of Rights and Constitution as separately paginated appendixes; and *Proceedings and Debates of the Virginia State Convention of 1829–30* (Richmond, Va., 1830); accounts are in Hugh Blair Grigsby, *The Virginia Convention of 1829–30* (Richmond, Va., 1854); Charles Henry Ambler, *Sectionalism in Virginia from 1776 to 1861* (Chicago, 1910), 147–70; George Brown Oliver, "A Constitutional History of Virginia, 1776–1860" (PhD diss., Duke University, 1959), 97–109; Merrill D. Peterson, *Democracy, Liberty, and Property: The State Constitutional Conventions of the 1820's* (Indianapolis, 1966), 271–85; Dickson D. Bruce Jr., *The Rhetoric of Conservatism: The Virginia Convention of 1829–30 and the Conservative Tradition in the South* (San Marino, Calif., 1982); Alison Goodyear Freehling, *Drift toward Dissolution: The Virginia Slavery Debate of 1831–1832* (Baton Rouge, La.,1982), 36–81; Robert P. Sutton, *Revolution to Secession: Constitution Making in the Old Dominion* (Charlottesville, Va., 1989), 72–102; Trenton E. Hizer, "'Virginia Is Now Divided': Politics in the Old Dominion, 1820–1833" (PhD diss., University of South Carolina, 1997), 221–68; Kevin R. C. Gutzman, *Virginia's American Revolution: From*

Dominion to Republic, 1776–1840 (Lanham, Md., 2007), 135–205; and Brent Tarter, *The Grandees of Government: The Origins and Persistence of Undemocratic Politics in Virginia* (Charlottesville, Va., 2013), 179–89.

2. *Acts of Assembly,* 1828–29 sess., chap. 15.

3. William Waller Hening, ed., *The Statutes at Large: Being a Collection of All the Laws of Virginia, from the First Session of the Legislature, in the Year 1619 . . . ,* 13 vols. (Richmond, Va., etc., 1809–23), 3:172–75.

4. Hening, *Statutes at Large,* 12:120.

5. Christopher M. Curtis, "Reconsidering Suffrage Reform in the 1829–1830 Virginia Constitutional Convention," *Journal of Southern History* 74 (2008): 89–124; see also, Christopher M. Curtis, *Jefferson's Freeholders and the Politics of Ownership in the Old Dominion* (New York, 2011).

6. Hening, *Statutes at Large,* 2:272–73.

7. Cf. Elmer C. Griffith, *The Rise and Development of the Gerrymander* (Chicago, 1907), 103–04, missed the importance of the 1782 tax law and misconstrued part of the 1817 Senate redistricting law and therefor doubted in 1907 that the changes in number of representatives and the franchise requirements of the Constitution of 1830 could be accurately described as a gerrymander or a deliberate manipulation of representation.

8. James E. Heath, *A Tabular Statement, Shewing the Free White, Free Coloured, Slave, and Total Population of Each County of the Commonwealth of Virginia, According to the Census of 1790, 1800, 1810, and 1820, Respectively; Prepared in Compliance with a Resolution of the Convention of Virginia, Passed on the 10th of October, 1829,* printed as Doc. No. 9 with *Journal, Acts and Proceedings of a General Convention.*

9. Constitution of the United States, Art. I, sec. 2, para. 3.

10. Virginia Constitution of 1970, Art. II, sec. 6.

11. *Journal, Acts and Proceedings,* 296–97.

12. Ambler, *Sectionalism in Virginia,* 172–74; Oliver, "Constitutional History," 110–14.

13. *Wheeling Gazette,* April 3, 1830.

14. Bruce, *Rhetoric of Conservatism,* 79–92; William G. Shade, *Democratizing the Old Dominion: Virginia and the Second Party System, 1824–1861* (Charlottesville, Va., 1996), 72–73; Tarter, *Grandees of Government,* 180–89.

6. The Great Gerrymander Revised and Disguised

1. Charles Henry Ambler, *Sectionalism in Virginia from 1776 to 1861* (Chicago, 1910), 252, derived from *Documents, Containing Statistics of*

Virginia; Ordered to Be Printed by the State Convention Sitting in the City of Richmond, 1850–51, and *Tables to Accompany Statement A. in the Report of the Committee on the Basis of Representation,* both bound with *Journal, Acts and Proceedings of a General Convention of the State of Virginia, Assembled at Richmond, on Monday, the Fourteenth Day of October, Eighteen Hundred and Fifty* (Richmond, Va., 1850 [i.e., 1851]).

2. Robert P. Sutton, *Revolution to Secession: Constitution Making in the Old Dominion* (Charlottesville, Va., 1989), 110–11; Brent Tarter, *The Grandees of Government: The Origins and Persistence of Undemocratic Politics in Virginia* (Charlottesville, Va., 2013), 180, 184, 189–90.

3. Kenneth W. Noe, *Southwest Virginia's Railroad: Modernization and the Sectional Crisis* (Urbana, Ill., 1994); Tarter, *Grandees of Government,* 203–06.

4. Ambler, *Sectionalism in Virginia,* 224–28, 240–44; Francis Pendleton Gaines, "The Virginia Constitutional Convention of 1850–51: A Study in Sectionalism" (PhD diss., University of Virginia, 1950), 70–73; Robin L. Einhorn, *American Taxation, American Slavery* (Chicago, 2006); Tarter, *Grandees of Government,* 191–92, 213–16; Paul E. Herron, *Framing the Solid South: The State Constitutional Conventions of Secession, Reconstruction, and Redemption, 1860–1902* (Lawrence, Kans., 2017), 44–64.

5. Laura J. Scalia, *America's Jeffersonian Experiment: Remaking State Constitutions, 1820–1850* (DeKalb, Ill., 1999), 134–46.

6. Tarter, *Grandees of Government,* 137–61, and sources cited 412–15; Patricia Hickin, "Anti-Slavery in Virginia, 1831–1861" (PhD diss., University of Virginia, 1968) is a remarkably thorough documentation of residual antislavery sentiment and activity in Virginia, but it may leave a false impression that antislavery thought retained greater political vitality after mid-century than in fact it did.

7. Lacy K. Ford, *Deliver Us from Evil: The Slavery Question in the Old South* (Oxford, 2009).

8. Ambler, *Sectionalism in Virginia,* 253–54; George Brown Oliver, "A Constitutional History of Virginia, 1776–1860" (PhD diss., Duke University, 1959), 118–19, 389–91.

9. *Proceedings of the Convention* printed with *Journal of the House of Delegates,* 1842–43 sess., as Doc. 29.

10. Gaines, "Virginia Constitutional Convention," 84; Oliver, "Constitutional History," 125–33.

11. *Acts of Assembly,* 1849–50 sess., chap. 8; *Statement Shewing the Data Upon Which Apportionment of Representation, in the Bill Concerning a*

Convention, Are Based, House Doc. 40, printed with *Journal of the House of Delegates,* 1849–1850 sess.; Gaines, "Virginia Constitutional Convention," 89–90; Tarter, *Grandees of Government,* 190.

12. *Journal of the House of Delegates,* 1849–50 sess., 261, 340 (quotation); *Journal of the Senate of Virginia,* 1849–50 sess., 126.

13. The convention's papers are in Records of the Convention of 1850–1851, Record Group 92, Library of Virginia, published in part in *Journal, Acts and Proceedings of a General Convention of the State of Virginia, Assembled at Richmond, on Monday, the Fourteenth Day of October, Eighteen Hundred and Fifty* (Richmond, Va., 1850 [i.e., 1851]); *Register of the Debates and Proceedings of the Va. Reform Convention* (Richmond, Va., 1851) includes reports for the dates January 6 through March 6, 1851 only; and surviving newspaper supplements in the Library of Virginia and at the College of William and Mary preserving some of the debates are incomplete. Scholarly accounts of the convention generally treat discussions of suffrage, representation, judicial reform, and other changes separately without a full narrative of the convention's work. Scholarly narratives are in Ambler, *Sectionalism in Virginia,* 261–70; Gaines, "The Virginia Constitutional Convention," 107–211, 227–76; Oliver, "Constitutional History of Virginia," 145–55, 308–15, 364–68, 389–408, 439–41; Sutton, *Revolution to Secession,* 122–36; Shade, *Democratizing the Old Dominion,* esp. 262–83; William A. Link, *Roots of Secession: Slavery and Politics in Antebellum Virginia* (Chapel Hill, N.C., 2003), 11–27, 73–74; and Tarter, *Grandees of Government,* 189–93.

14. Gaines, "Virginia Constitutional Convention," 227–51; Oliver, "Constitutional History of Virginia," 439–41; Sutton, *Revolution to Secession,* 134–36.

15. Tarter, *Grandees of Government,* 189–93.

16. Cf. the slightly different tabulation in Gaines, "Virginia Constitutional Convention," 211.

17. *McCulloch v. The State of Maryland,* 17 US 316 (1819), quotation on 331.

18. John E. Stealey III, *West Virginia's Civil War–Era Constitution: Loyal Revolution, Confederate Counter-Revolution, and the Convention of 1872* (Kent, Ohio, 2013); 34–35; Tarter, *Grandees of Government,* 213–16.

19. Charles H. Ambler, Frances Haney Atwood, and William B. Mathews, eds., *Debates and Proceedings of the First Constitutional Convention of West Virginia (1861–1863),* 3 vols. (Huntington, W.Va., 1939), with text of constitution and implementation schedule at 3:859–88; Stealey, *West Virginia's Civil War–Era Constitution,* 72–106.

7. Disfranchisement Replaces the Great Gerrymander

1. Records of the Virginia Convention of 1864, Record Group 95, Library of Virginia; *Journal of the Constitutional Convention Which Convened at Alexandria on the 13th Day of February, 1864* (Alexandria, Va., 1864); *Constitution of the State of Virginia, and the Ordinances Adopted by the Convention Which Assembled at Alexandria, on the 13th Day of February, 1864* (Alexandria, Va., 1864); the official enrolled parchment of the Constitution of 1864 is in the Virginia Historical Society old catalog record Mss13:1864 Apr 7:1; Sara B. Bearss, "'Restored and Vindicated': The Virginia Constitutional Convention of 1864," *Virginia Magazine of History and Biography* 122 (2014): 156–81.

2. Records of the Convention of 1867–1868, Record Group 96, Library of Virginia, including authenticated enrolled parchment constitution; *Journal of the Constitutional Convention of the State of Virginia* (Richmond, Va., 1868); only a partial edition of the planned published debates appeared in print as *Debates and Proceedings of the Constitutional Convention of the State of Virginia* (Richmond, Va., 1868); *Documents of the Constitutional Convention;* the little scholarly literature on the convention focuses almost entirely on the delegates: Richard G. Lowe, "Virginia's Reconstruction Convention: General Schofield Rates the Delegates," *Virginia Magazine of History and Biography* 80 (1972): 341–60; Richard L. Hume, "The Membership of the Virginia Constitutional Convention of 1867–1868: A Study of the Beginnings of Congressional Reconstruction in the Upper South," *Virginia Magazine of History and Biography* 86 (1978): 461–84; Richard L. Hume and Jerry B. Gouch, *Blacks, Carpetbaggers, and Scalawags: The Constitutional Conventions of Radical Reconstruction* (Baton Rouge, La., 2008).

3. *Acts of Assembly,* 1870–71 sess., chap. 162, and 1871–72 sess., chap. 195.

4. 39th Cong., 2d sess., chap. 63; 40th Cong., 1st sess., chap. 6, and Joint Res. 40.

5. Records of the General Assembly, Record Group 87, Library of Virginia, Enrolled Bills, 1875–76 sess., chap. 87; ratification by vote of 129,373 to 98,359 certified in Secretary of the Commonwealth Election Record No. 109, Record Group 13, Library of Virginia but with a notation that 360 votes in favor of the amendment and 383 votes opposed to it from Prince George County were "rejected."

6. Pippa Holloway, "'A Chicken-Stealer Shall Lose His Vote': Disfranchisement for Larceny in the South, 1874–1890," *Journal of Southern History*

75 (2009): 931–62; see also Pippa Holloway, *Living in Infamy: Felon Disfranchisement and the History of American Citizenship* (New York, 2014).

7. Brent Tarter, *A Saga of the New South: Race, Law, and Public Debt in Virginia* (Charlottesville, Va., 2016), 40–41; Tarter, "African Americans and Politics in Virginia (1865–1902)," Virginia Humanities online *Encyclopedia Virginia* (2015).

8. Enrolled Bills, 1881–82 sess., chap. 78; ratification by vote of 107,303 to 66,131 certified in Secretary of the Commonwealth Election Record No. 104.

9. Charles E. Wynes, *Race Relations in Virginia, 1870–1902* (Charlottesville, Va., 1961); Ronald E. Shibley, "Election Laws and Electoral Practices in Virginia, 1867–1902" (PhD diss., University of Virginia, 1972), esp. 60–214; Wythe Holt, *Virginia's Constitutional Convention of 1901–1902* (New York, 1990); Brent Tarter, *The Grandees of Government: The Origins and Persistence of Undemocratic Politics in Virginia* (Charlottesville, Va., 2013), 262–65; Tarter, "African Americans and Politics in Virginia"; Tarter, "The Republican Party in the Nineteenth Century," Virginia Humanities online *Encyclopedia Virginia* (2014).

10. *Acts of Assembly,* 1884 special sess., chap. 158.

11. Shibley, "Election Laws and Electoral Practices in Virginia," esp. 60–215; Holt, *Virginia's Constitutional Convention,* 59–74; Tarter, *Grandees of Government,* 264–68.

12. *Acts of Assembly,* 1893–94 sess., chap. 746.

13. *Daily State Journal* [Richmond], April 24, 1871.

14. Michael B. Chesson, "Richmond's Black Councilmen, 1871–1896," in *Southern Black Leaders of the Reconstruction Era,* ed. Howard N. Rabinowitz (Urbana, Ill., 1982), 216; Michel B. Chesson, *Richmond after the War, 1865–1890* (Richmond, Va., 1981), 192–93.

15. Winnett W. Hagens, "The Politics of Race: The Virginia Redistricting Experience, 1991–1997," in *Race and Redistricting in the 1990s,* ed. Bernard Grofman (New York, 1998), 319.

16. Records of the Convention of 1901–1902, Record Group 97, Library of Virginia; *Journal of the Constitutional Convention of Virginia Held in the City of Richmond, Beginning June 12th, 1901* (Richmond, Va., 1901 [i.e., 1902]); *Report of the Proceedings and Debates of the Constitutional Convention State of Virginia Held in the City of Richmond June 12, 1901, to June 26, 1902,* 2 vols. (Richmond, Va., 1906); Julian A. C. Chandler, "Constitutional

Revision in Virginia," *Proceedings of the American Political Science Association, Fifth Annual Meeting* (1909): 192–202; John W. Daniel, "The Work of the Constitutional Convention," *Reports of the Virginia State Bar Association* 15 (1902): 257–94; Wythe Holt, "The Virginia Constitutional Convention of 1901–1902: A Reform Movement Which Lacked Substance," *Virginia Magazine of History and Biography* 76 (1968): 67–102; Holt, *Virginia's Constitutional Convention;* Ralph C. McDanel, *The Virginia Constitutional Convention of 1901–1902* (Baltimore, 1928); Tarter, *Grandees of Government,* 265–72.

17. Tarter, *Grandees of Government,* 266, 267, 271–72.

18. *Report of the Proceedings and Debates,* 2:2975.

19. *Report of the Proceedings and Debates,* 2:3014.

20. Lila Meade Valentine to Jessie Townsend, April 1, 1915, and to Mary Elizabeth Pidgeon, October 11, 1919, both in Equal Suffrage League Records, Library of Virginia.

21. *Report of the Proceedings and Debates,* 2:3076–77.

22. Herman L. Horn, "The Growth and Development of the Democratic Party in Virginia since 1890" (PhD diss., Duke University, 1949), 102–13.

23. Tarter, *Grandees of Government,* 296–304; V. O. Key, *Southern Politics in State and Nation* (New York, 1949), 17–33.

24. Key, *Southern Politics in State and Nation;* Horn, "The Growth and Development of the Democratic Party"; Charles E. Wynes, *Race Relations in Virginia, 1870–1902* (Charlottesville, Va., 1961); Andrew Buni, *The Negro in Virginia Politics, 1902–1965* (Charlottesville, Va., 1967); Allen W. Moger, *Virginia: Bourbonism to Byrd, 1870–1925* (Charlottesville, Va., 1968); Raymond H. Pulley, *Old Virginia Restored: An Interpretation of the Progressive Impulse, 1870–1930* (Charlottesville, Va., 1968); J. Harvie Wilkinson III, *Harry Byrd and the Changing Face of Virginia Politics, 1945–1966* (Charlottesville, Va., 1968); Larry J. Sabato, *The Democratic Party Primary in Virginia: Tantamount to Election No Longer* (Charlottesville, Va., 1977); Ronald L. Heinemann, *Depression and New Deal in Virginia: The Enduring Dominion* (Charlottesville, Va., 1983); Paul T. Murray, "Who Is an Indian; Who Is a Negro: Virginia Indians in the World War II Draft," *Virginia Magazine of History and Biography* 956 (1987): 215–31; Richard B. Sherman, "The 'Teachings at Hampton Institute': Social Equality, Racial Integrity, and the Virginia Public Assemblage Act of 1926," *Virginia Magazine of History and Biography* 95 (1987): 275–300; Richard B. Sherman, "'The Last Stand':

The Fight for Racial Integrity in Virginia in the 1920s," *Journal of Southern History* 54 (1988): 69–92; Holt, *Virginia's Constitutional Convention of 1901–1902;* Ronald L. Heinemann, *Harry Byrd of Virginia* (Charlottesville, Va., 1996); Winnett W. Hagens, "The Politics of Race: The Virginia Redistricting Experience, 1991–1997," in *Race and Redistricting in the 1990s,* ed. Bernard Grofman (New York, 1998), 315–19; J. Douglas Smith, *Managing White Supremacy: Race, Politics, and Citizenship in Jim Crow Virginia* (Chapel Hill, N.C., 2002); Pippa Holloway, *Sexuality, Politics, and Social Control in Virginia, 1920–1945* (Chapel Hill, N.C., 2006); Arica L. Coleman, *That the Blood Stay Pure: African Americans, Native Americans, and the Predicament of Race and Identity in Virginia* (Bloomington, Ind., 2013); Tarter, *Grandees of Government;* William P. Hustwit, *James J. Kilpatrick: Salesman for Segregation* (Chapel Hill, N.C., 2013); Julian Maxwell Hayter, *The Dream Is Lost: Voting Rights and the Politics of Race in Richmond, Virginia* (Lexington, Ky., 2017).

8. Malapportionment in the Twentieth Century

1. *Brown v. Saunders,* 159 VA 31 (1932), quotation on 43.

2. Ralph Eisenberg, "Legislative Apportionment: How Representative Is Virginia's Present System?" *University of Virginia News Letter* 37 (April 15, 1961): 29; and Ralph H. Eisenberg, "Legislative Reapportionment and Congressional Redistricting in Virginia," *Washington and Lee Law Review* 23 (1966): 300–02.

3. Jean Gottmann, *Virginia at Mid-Century* (New York 1955); Lorin A. Thompson, "Recent Population Changes in Virginia," *University of Virginia News Letter* 37 (February 15, 1961): 21–24; Thompson, "Virginia Population Changes: Age and Color, 1960 and 1970," *University of Virginia News Letter* 37 (June 15, 1961): 37–40; Paul Theodore David and Ralph Eisenberg, *Devaluation of the Urban and Suburban Votes: A Statistical Investigation of Long-Term Trends in State Legislative Representation,* 2 vols. (Charlottesville, Va., 1961–62), 1:2–3, 4–7, 64–65, and 2:164–70.

4. J. Douglas Smith, "'When Reason Collides with Prejudice': Armistead Lloyd Boothe and the Politics of Moderation," in *The Moderates' Dilemma: Massive Resistance to School Desegregation in Virginia,* ed. Matthew D. Lassiter and Andrew B. Lewis (Charlottesville, Va., 1998), 28–29; *Opinions of the Attorney General and Report to the Governor of Virginia from July 1, 1951 to June 30, 1952* (Richmond, Va., 1952), 85; MS Handbook of Redistricting the Senate

and House of Delegates of Virginia 1952, copy in Armistead Lloyd Boothe Papers, University of Virginia; *Alexandria Gazette,* May 24 (quoting Boothe), September 17, 18, 1952; *Acts of Assembly,* 1952 special sess., chaps. 17, 18.

5. Manning J. Dauer and Robert G. Kelsay, "Unrepresentative States," *National Municipal Review* 44 (1955): 571–75, 587; Eisenberg, "Legislative Apportionment," 29–30.

6. J. Douglas Smith, *On Democracy's Doorstep: The Inside Story of How the Supreme Court Brought "One Person, One Vote" to the United States* (New York, 2014), 151, 287–90.

7. Eisenberg, "Legislative Apportionment," 30–31.

8. Eisenberg, "Legislative Apportionment," 31–32; Eisenberg, "Legislative Reapportionment and Congressional Redistricting," 301.

9. Benjamin Muse, *Virginia's Massive Resistance* (Bloomington, Ind., 1961), 30–31; Smith, *Doorstep of Democracy,* 19. I thank J. Douglas Smith for pointing out to me that Muse was correct according to the 1960 census, but not according to the 1950 census, which suggests that his estimate was probably close to correct midway between them.

10. *Acts of Assembly,* 1883–84 sess., chap. 147.

11. *Wise v. Bigger,* 97 VA 269 (1884), quotation on 282.

12. *Acts of Assembly,* 1932 sess., chap. 23.

13. Pamela S. Karlan, "Reapportionment, Nonapportionment, and Recovering some Lost History of One Person, One Vote," *William and Mary Law Review* 59 (2018): 1921–59.

14. *Brown v. Saunders,* 159 VA 31 (1932), quotations on 45, 46.

9. The Representation Revolution of the 1960s

1. *Colegrove v. Green,* 328 US 549 (1946), quotation on 556.

2. *Baker v. Carr,* 369 US 186 (1962).

3. *Gray v. Sanders,* 372 US 368 (1963), quotation on 381.

4. *Reynolds v. Sims,* 377 US 533 (1964), quotations on 555 and 562.

5. *Reynolds v. Sims,* 377 US 533 (1964), 578, 579.

6. *Wesberry v. Sanders,* 376 US 1 (1964); *WMCA v. Lomenzo,* 377 US 633 (1964); *Maryland Committee for Fair Representation v. Tawes,* 377 US 656 (1964); *Davis v. Mann,* 377 US 678 (1964); *Roman v. Sincock,* 377 US 695 (1964); *Lucas v. Forty-Fourth General Assembly of Colorado,* 377 US 715 (1964); *Avery v. Midland County, Texas,* 390 US 474 (1968); *Hadley v. Junior College District of Metropolitan Kansas City,* 397 US 50 (1970).

7. *Harper v. Virginia State Board of Elections,* 383 US 663 (1966).

8. 89th Cong., 1st sess., chap. 110.

9. A. E. Dick Howard et al., *Report of the Commission on Constitutional Revision . . .* (Charlottesville, Va., 1969); *Proceedings and Debates of the Virginia House of Delegates Pertaining to Amendment of the Constitution, Extra Session 1969, Regular Session 1970* (Richmond, Va., 1970); *Proceedings and Debates of the Senate of Virginia Pertaining to Amendment of the Constitution: Extra Session 1969, Regular Session 1970* (Richmond, Va., 1970); A. E. Dick Howard, "Constitutional Revision: Virginia and the Nation," *University of Richmond Law Review* 9 (1974): 1–48; A. E. Dick Howard, *Commentaries on the Constitution of Virginia,* 2 vols. (Charlottesville, Va., 1974).

10. Thomas R. Morris and Neil Bradley, "Virginia," in *Quiet Revolution in the South: The Impact of the Voting Rights Act, 1965–1990,* ed. Chandler Davidson and Bernard Grofman (Princeton, N.J., 1994), 275–77.

11. Leroy Hardy, *The Gerrymander: Origin, Conception and Re-emergence* (Claremont, Calif., 1990).

10. The Representation Revolution in Virginia

1. *Acts of Assembly,* 1962 sess., chaps. 635, 638.

2. *Mann v. Davis,* 213 F. Supp. 577 (1962); Ralph Eisenberg, "Legislative Reapportionment and Congressional Redistricting in Virginia," *Washington and Lee Law Review* 23 (1966): 302–08.

3. *Davis v. Mann,* 377 US 678 (1964), quotation on 690; Eisenberg, "Legislative Reapportionment and Congressional Redistricting," 308–11; J. Douglas Smith, *On Democracy's Doorstep: The Inside Story of How the Supreme Court Brought "One Person, One Vote" to the United States* (New York, 2014), 140–41, 184–86; Micah Altman and Michael P. McDonald, "A Half-Century of Virginia Redistricting Battles: Shifting from Rural Malapportionment to Voting Rights to Public Participation," *University of Richmond Law Review* 47 (2013): 779–82.

4. *Mann v. Davis,* 238 F. Supp. 458 (1964).

5. *Acts of Assembly,* 1964 special sess., chaps. 1, 2; Eisenberg, "Legislative Reapportionment and Congressional Redistricting," 312.

6. *Mann v. Davis,* 245 F. Supp. 241 (1965); Eisenberg, "Legislative Reapportionment and Congressional Redistricting," 313–17.

7. *Mann v. Davis,* 245 F. Supp. 241 (1965), quotation on 245; Eisenberg, "Legislative Reapportionment and Congressional Redistricting," 312–17.

8. *Acts of Assembly,* 1952 sess., chap. 282.

9. *Wilkins v. Davis,* 205 VA 803 (1965); *Acts of Assembly,* 1965 special sess., chap. 1; Eisenberg, "Legislative Reapportionment and Congressional Redistricting," 317–23.

10. *Acts of Assembly,* 1971 special sess., chap. 118.

11. Unpublished order of *Simpson v. Mahan* reported in detail in the *News Leader* [Richmond] and *Richmond Times-Dispatch,* both March 2, 1972.

12. *Acts of Assembly,* 1972 sess., chap. 21.

13. Robert J. Austin, "Congressional Redistricting in Virginia: Political Implications of One Man–One Vote," *University of Virginia News Letter* 48 (July 15, 1972): 41–44; *Kirkpatrick v. Preisler,* 394 US 526 (1969).

14. *Acts of Assembly,* 1971 special sess., chaps. 116, 120, 246; Robert Jackson Austin, "The Redistricting Process after One Man–One Vote: The Case of Virginia" (PhD diss., University of Virginia, 1976).

15. *Mahan v. Howell,* 410 US 315 (1973), quotation on 318, 319n6, 324, 330–32.

16. *Howell v. Mahan,* 330 F. Supp. 138 (1971) on 1146–47.

17. *Mahan v. Howell,* 410 US 315 (1973) on 331–332.

18. *Howell v. Mahan,* 330 F. Supp. 1138 (1971) on 1145.

19. *Mahan v. Howell,* 410 US 315 (1973), quotations on 328, 329.

20. *Mahan v. Howell,* 410 US 315 (1973), 333; Altman and McDonald, "A Half-Century of Virginia Redistricting Battles," 782–85.

21. Murel M. Jones Jr., "The Impact of Annexation-related City Council Reapportionment on Black Political Influence: The Cities of Richmond and Petersburg, Virginia" (PhD diss., Howard University, 1977).

22. Chester W. Bain, "Annexation: The Virginia Procedure," *University of Virginia News Letter* 37 (1961): 41–44.

23. *Petersburg v. United States,* 354 F. Supp. 1021 (1972), quotation on 1028.

24. *City of Richmond v. United States,* 422 US 358 (1975), quotation on 364.

25. *Holt v. City of Richmond,* 334 F. Supp. 228 (1971).

26. *City of Richmond v. Holt,* 459 F. 2d. 1093 (1972).

27. *City of Richmond v. United States,* 422 US 358 (1975); John V. Moeser and Rutledge M. Dennis, *The Politics of Annexation: Oligarchic Power in a Southern City* (Cambridge, Mass., 1982); Julian Maxwell Hayter, *The Dream Is Lost: Voting Rights and the Politics of Race in Richmond, Virginia* (Lexington, Ky., 2017), 111–50.

28. Thomas R. Morris and Neil Bradley, "Virginia," in *Quiet Revolution in the South: The Impact of the Voting Rights Act, 1965–1990,* ed. Chandler Davidson and Bernard Grofman (Princeton, N.J., 1994), 282–98.

29. *Acts of Assembly,* 1981 special sess., chaps. 2, 14 (the several acts of the several special sessions in 1981 were all printed together and distinguished by the date of adoption); Frank R. Parker, "The Virginia Legislative Reapportionment Case: Reapportionment Issues of the 1980's," *George Mason University Law Review* 5 (1982): 12–16.

30. *Acts of Assembly,* 1981 special sess., chap. 5.

31. *Acts of Assembly,* 1981 special sess., chap. 12; F.B.A., "The Reapportionment Dilemma: Lessons from the Virginia Experience," *Virginia Law Review* 68 (1982): 550–52; Parker, "The Virginia Legislative Reapportionment Case," 1–12; Frank R. Parker, "Racial Gerrymandering and Legislative Reapportionment," in *Minority Vote Dilution,* ed. Chandler Davidson (Washington, D.C., 1984), 88–98; John G. Schuiteman and John G. Selph, "The 1981/1982 Reapportionment of the Virginia House of Delegates," *University of Virginia News Letter* 59 (June 1983): 47–51; Altman and McDonald, "Half-Century of Virginia Redistricting Battles," 785–87.

32. *Cosner v. Dalton,* 522 F. Supp. 350 (1981), quotation on 359; F.B.A., "Reapportionment Dilemma," 552–64; Parker, "Virginia Legislative Reapportionment."

33. *Acts of Assembly,* 1981 special sess., chap. 16, veto message and quotation on 82.

34. *Acts of Assembly,* 1982 special sess., chap. 1.

35. Parker, "Virginia Legislative Reapportionment," 48.

36. *Acts of Assembly,* 1982 special sess., chap. 1.

11. Partisan Redistricting

1. Winnett W. Hagens, "Redistricting the Commonwealth: A Narrative and Analysis of the Virginia Outcome, 1991–1996," in *Race and Representation,* ed. Georgia A. Persons (New Brunswick N.J., 1997), 44–62; Winnett W. Hagens, "The Politics of Race: The Virginia Redistricting Experience, 1991–1997," in *Race and Redistricting in the 1990s,* ed. Bernard Grofman (New York, 1998), 319–25; Kenneth S. Stroupe Jr., "Gerrymandering's Long History in Virginia: Will This Decade Mark the End?" *Virginia News Letter* 85 (February 1, 2009); Micah Altman and Michael P. McDonald, "A Half-Century of Virginia Redistricting Battles: Shifting from Rural Malapportionment to Voting Rights to Public Participation," *University of Richmond Law Review* 47 (2013): 787–90.

2. *Acts of Assembly,* 1991 special sess., chap. 11; Hagens, "The Politics of Race," 325.

3. *Davis v. Bandemer,* 478 US 109 (1986).

4. *Republican Party of Virginia v. Wilder,* 774 F. Supp. 400 (1991); Hagens, "The Politics of Race," 325–27.

5. *Acts of Assembly,* 1991 special sess., chap. 18; Hagens, "The Politics of Race," 327–28.

6. *Jamerson v. Womack,* 244 VA 506 (1992), quotation on 517.

7. *Acts of Assembly,* 1991 second special sess., chap. 6; Hagens, "The Politics of Race," 328–29; Stroupe, "Gerrymandering's Long History."

8. *Moon v. Meadows,* 952 F. Sup. 1141 (1997), quotations on 1142, 1147.

9. *Acts of Assembly,* 1998 sess., chap. 1.

10. *Acts of Assembly,* 2001 sess., chap. 7.

11. *Page v. Virginia State Board of Elections,* 58 F. Supp. 3d 533 (2014), and *Page v. Virginia State Board of Elections,* No. 3:13cvb678 (2015).

12. *Acts of Assembly,* 1998 sess., chap. 1; *Personhuballah v. Alcorn,* 239 F. Supp. 3d 929 (2016).

13. Altman and McDonald, "Half-Century of Virginia Redistricting Battles," 790–92.

14. *Richmond Times-Dispatch,* February 21, 2017, is one of many instances in which Schapiro used the phrase.

15. *Wilkins v. West,* 447 VA 103 (2002), quotation on 118.

16. *Hall v. Virginia,* 385 F. Supp. 3d 421 (2004).

17. *Acts of Assembly,* 2011 special sess., chap. 1. Benjamin M. Harris and Stephen J. Farnsworth, "With Overwhelming Support for Nonpartisan Redistricting, Virginians Are Studying Ways to Make That Happen," *Virginia News Letter* 90 (June 2014); Geoffrey Skelley, "Virginia's Redistricting History: What's Past Is Prologue," on *Sabato's Crystal Ball* (June 18, 2015), available online at http://www.centerforpolitics.org/crystalball/articles/virginias-redistricting-history-whats-past-is-prologue; Jeff Thomas, *Virginia Politics and Government in a New Century: The Price of Power* (Charleston, S.C., 2016), 42–48.

18. For a brief, clear synopsis, see Christopher S. Elmendorf, "From Educational Adequacy to Representational Adequacy: A New Template for Legal Attacks on Partisan Gerrymanders," *William and Mary Law Review* 59 (2018): 1648–56.

19. Altman and McDonald, "Half-Century of Virginia Redistricting Battles," 792–828.

20. *Vesilind v. Virginia State Board of Elections et al.,* VA Record No. 170697 (2018).

21. *Brown v. Saunders,* 159 VA 31 (1932).

22. For an early summary of compactness measurement, see Daniel D. Polsby and Robert D. Popper, "The Third Criterion: Compactness as Procedural Safeguard against Partisan Gerrymandering," *Yale Law and Policy Review* 9 (1991): 326–53; for a description of alternative methods applied in the Virginia case, see *Vesilind v. Virginia State Board of Elections et al.,* VA Record No. 170697 (2018).

23. Richard L. Hasen, "Race or Party, Race as Party, or Party all the Time: Three Uneasy Approaches to Conjoined Polarization in Redistricting and Voting Cases," *William and Mary Law Review* 59 (2018): 1843–64; Ellen D. Katz, "Section 2 after Section 5: Voting Rights and the Race to the Bottom," *William and Mary Law Review* 59 (2018): 1962–91.

24. Summarized at length in *Bethune-Hill v. Virginia State Board of Elections,* 141 F. Supp. 3d 505 (2015) and in *Bethune-Hill v. Virginia State Board of Elections,* Civil Action 3:14cv852 (2018).

25. *Bethune-Hill v. Virginia State Board of Elections,* 141 F. Supp. 3d 505 (2015).

26. *Alabama Legislative Black Caucus v. Alabama,* 575 US doc. no. 13–859 (2015).

27. *Bethune-Hill v. Virginia State Board of Elections,* 580 US No. 15–680 (2017).

28. *Bethune-Hill v. Virginia State Board of Elections,* Civil Action 3:14cv852 (2018).

29. *Richmond Times-Dispatch,* August 31, 2018.

30. *Richmond Times-Dispatch,* November 14, 2018.

31. *Richmond Times-Dispatch,* September 28, 2018.

32. *Richmond Times-Dispatch,* October 6, 2018.

33. *Virginia House of Delegates et al. v. Bethune-Hill et al.*, 587 US No. 18–281 (2019); *Richmond Times-Dispatch*, February 15, June 18, 2019.

34. Hagens, "The Politics of Race," 322–33; Nicholas O. Stephanopolous, "The Causes and Consequences of Gerrymandering," *William and Mary Law Review* 59 (2018): 2115–58.

35. Stephen Hanna and Stephen J. Farnsworth, "Visualizing Virginia's Changing Electorate: Mapping Presidential Elections from 2000 to 2012," *Virginia News Letter* 89 (May 2013).

36. For a summary of recent legislation and litigation to discourage voting, see Dale E. Ho, "Something Old, Something New, or Something *Really* Old? Second-Generation Racial Gerrymandering Litigation as Intentional Racial Discrimination Cases," *William and Mary Law Review* 59 (2018): 1903–8; testimony and other evidence introduced at trials to test the validity of some of those laws is available online at https://brennancenter.org in the elections and voting rights portion of the New York University School of Law's Brennan Center for Justice.

12. The Political and Legal Landscapes in Virginia in 2019

1. *Shelby County v. Holder,* 570 US 2 (2013).

2. Daniel P. Tokaji, "Gerrymandering and Association," *William and Mary Law Review* 59 (2018): 2160–209, esp. 2177–90.

3. Bruce E. Cain, Wendy K. Tam Cho, Yan Y. Liu, and Emily R. Zhang, "A Reasonable Bias Approach to Gerrymandering: Using Automated Plan Generation to Evaluate Redistricting Proposals," *William and Mary Law Review* 59 (2018): 1521–57; Edward B. Foley, "The Gerrymander and the Constitution: Two Avenues of Analysis and the Quest for a Durable Precedent," *William and Mary Law Review* 59 (2018): 1729–85, esp. 1729–51.

4. Michael Parsons, "Clearing the Political Thicket: Why Political Gerrymandering for Partisan Advantage Is Unconstitutional," *William and Mary Bill of Rights Journal* 24 (2016): 1107–67.

5. *Whitford v. Gill,* 218 F. Supp. 3d 837 (2016).

6. *Gill v. Whitford,* 585 US No. 16–1161 (2018).

7. *Benisek v. Lamone,* 582 US (2018).

8. *Common Cause et al. v. Rucho,* Middle District of North Carolina 1:16-CV-1026 and 1:16-CV-1164.

9. *League of Women Voters et al. v. Pennsylvania,* 159 MM 2017 (2018).

10. Brent Tarter, "The Virginia Declaration of Rights," in *To Secure the Blessing of Liberty: Rights in American History,* ed. Josephine F. Pacheco (Fairfax, Va., 1993), 49.

11. Record of the case online at https://www.brennancenter.org/legal-work/league-women-voters-v-pennslyvania accessed August 30, 2018.

12. Benjamin M. Harris and Stephen J. Farnsworth, "With Overwhelming Support for Nonpartisan Redistricting, Virginians Are Studying Ways to Make That Happen," *Virginia News Letter* 90 (June 2014); *Richmond*

Times-Dispatch, August 31, 2018; and statement by the chair of the committee, Wyatt Durrette, "If Pols Were Angels, No Reform Would be Necessary," *Richmond Times-Dispatch,* September 25, 2018.

13. Peter Miller and Bernard Grofman, "Redistricting Commissions in the Western United States," *University of California Irvine Law Review* 3 (2013): 637–68.

14. SJR 306, 2019 sess.; *Richmond Times-Dispatch,* February 24, 2019.

FOR FURTHER INFORMATION

Histories of redistricting, reapportionment, and gerrymandering, some with special emphasis on Virginia, include:

Elmer C. Griffith, *The Rise and Development of the Gerrymander* (Chicago, 1907) is the earliest scholarly investigation of gerrymandering in the United States and carries its analysis up to 1840. It is available online through Google Books.

J. R. Pole, "Representation and Authority in Virginia from the Revolution to Reform," *Journal of Southern History* 24 (1958): 16–50 clearly explains the relationship between representation and property from the colonial period through the Constitutional Convention of 1850–51.

Ralph [H.] Eisenberg, "Legislative Apportionment: How Representative Is Virginia's Present System?" *University of Virginia News Letter* 37 (April 15, 1961): 29–32 analyzes malapportionment in Virginia in the middle of the twentieth century and describes some of the methods by which political scientists then measured malapportionment.

Ralph H. Eisenberg, "Legislative Reapportionment and Congressional Redistricting in Virginia," *Washington and Lee Law Review* 23 (1966): 295–323 thoroughly analyzes the first court cases the representation revolution generated in Virginia.

Robert J. Austin, "Congressional Redistricting in Virginia: Political Implications of One Man–One Vote," *University of Virginia News Letter* 48 (July 15, 1972): 41–44 is a concise account of the first redistricting in Virginia following the representation revolution of the 1960s.

Frank R. Parker, "The Virginia Legislative Reapportionment Case: Reapportionment Issues of the 1980's," *George Mason University Law Review* 5 (1982): 1–50 analyzes the 1981–82 redistricting sessions of the General Assembly.

F.B.A., "The Reapportionment Dilemma: Lessons from the Virginia Experience," *Virginia Law Review* 68 (1982): 541–70 is a thoughtful discussion of the implications of the representation revolution and the 1981–82 redistricting sessions of the General Assembly.

John G. Schuiteman and John G. Selph, "The 1981/1982 Reapportionment of the Virginia House of Delegates," *University of Virginia News Letter* 59 (June 1983): 47–51 is a brief but useful summary of the 1981–82 redistricting sessions of the General Assembly.

Frank R. Parker, "Racial Gerrymandering and Legislative Reapportionment," in *Minority Vote Dilution,* edited by Chandler Davidson (Washington, D.C., 1984), 85–117 carefully extracts racial motivations from the complex mix of partisan issues at work during the 1981–82 redistricting sessions of the General Assembly.

Thomas R. Morris and Neil Bradley, "Virginia," in *Quiet Revolution in the South: The Impact of the Voting Rights Act, 1965–1990,* edited by Chandler Davidson and Bernard Grofman (Princeton, N.J., 1994), 271–98 is an important account of how the Voting Rights Act changed electoral politics in Virginia. The volume also contains essays on how the Voting Rights Act changed the politics of redistricting and reapportionment in each of the other southern states.

Winnett W. Hagens, "Redistricting the Commonwealth: A Narrative and Analysis of the Virginia Outcome, 1991–1996," in *Race and Representation,* edited by Georgia A. Persons (New Brunswick N.J., 1997), 44–62 and Winnett W. Hagens, "The Politics of Race: The Virginia Redistricting Experience, 1991–1997," in *Race and Redistricting in the 1990s,* edited by Bernard Grofman (New York, 1998), 315–42 are fine accounts of race and the partisanship of redistricting in the 1991 session of the General Assembly and its immediate aftermath. Both volumes contain other essays on the politics of race and redistricting in the 1980s and 1990s.

Gary W. Cox and Jonathan Katz, *Elbridge Gerry's Salamander* (Cambridge, U.K., 2002) evaluates the effects of the representation revolution of the 1960s on members of Congress and candidates for Congress from outside the southern states.

Justin Levitt and Erika Wood, "A Citizen's Guide to Redistricting" (2008) is a handy compilation of data and contains a glossary of terms and has been available through the New York University School of Law's Brennan Center for Justice free online at https://brennancenter.org since 2010.

Kenneth S. Stroupe Jr., "Gerrymandering's Long History in Virginia: Will This Decade Mark the End?" *Virginia News Letter* 85 (February 1, 2009) is a brief, useful account of late twentieth- and early twenty-first-century redistricting in Virginia.

Brent Tarter, *The Grandees of Government: The Origins and Persistence of Undemocratic Politics in Virginia* (Charlottesville, Va., 2013) is an extended account of the political culture of Virginia from the beginnings of the colonial period to the second decade of the twenty-first century. The subtitle indicates what the book is about, the title tells who done it.

Micah Altman and Michael P. McDonald, "A Half-Century of Virginia Redistricting Battles: Shifting from Rural Malapportionment to Voting Rights to Public Participation," *University of Richmond Law Review* 47 (2013): 771–831, despite a weak and in some particulars inaccurate account of pre–one person, one vote redistricting, describes late twentieth- and early twenty-first-century partisan redistricting and includes a long section on student participation in the 2011 redistricting of the House of Representatives and the General Assembly.

Erik J. Engstrom, *Partisan Gerrymandering and the Construction of American Democracy* (Ann Arbor, Mich., 2013) concentrates on congressional gerrymandering from 1840 to the present.

J. Douglas Smith, *On Democracy's Doorstep: The Inside Story of How the Supreme Court Brought "One Person, One Vote" to the United States* (New York, 2014) is an excellent account of the legal and political battles that led to the one person, one vote decision in 1963 in *Gray v. Saunders* and its immediate aftermath.

Peter F. Galderisi, ed., *Redistricting in the New Millennium* (Lanham, Md., 2015) summarizes much of the early twenty-first-century literature and court cases.

Geoffrey Skelley, "Virginia's Redistricting History: What's Past Is Prologue" on *Sabato's Crystal Ball* (June 18, 2015), available online at http://www.centerforpolitics.org/crystalball/articles/virginias-redistricting-history-whats-past-is-prologue gives a good account of the state of Virginia's 2011 Senate, House of Delegates, and House of Representatives districts and the litigation underway as of the summer of 2015.

Michael Parsons, "Clearing the Political Thicket: Why Political Gerrymandering for Partisan Advantage Is Unconstitutional," *William and Mary Bill of Rights Journal* 24 (2016): 1107–67 clearly summarizes all the complex legal issues partisan gerrymandering presents.

William and Mary Law Review 59, no. 5 (April 2018) contains fifteen substantial articles covering more than 750 pages that analyze almost all aspects of redistricting law and the scholarly literature as of that time.

Useful Online Resources

The Gerrymandering Project's website at project.fivethirtyeight.com monitors congressional redistricting, including for Virginia.

The Ballotpedia website at ballotpedia.org compiles and publishes up-to-date data on redistricting.

All decisions of the Supreme Court of the United States are available free online at https://supreme.justia.com/cases/federal/us/

including so-called "slip opinions" of the most-recent decisions that have been issued but not yet compiled and bound in the official volumes of *United States Reports.*

Appellate court decisions in all important twenty-first-century redistricting cases are available online at New York University School of Law's Brennan Center for Justice at https://brennancenter.org and in some instances include exhibits, testimony, and other submissions that describe in detail the various computational techniques by which experts assessed and applied population data, measured deviations from least- to most-populous districts, and evaluated compactness, partisanship, and other characteristics.

In the past the United States Census Bureau, the General Assembly of Virginia, and the Weldon Cooper Center for Public Service at the University of Virginia at coopercenter.org have published or posted census data configured for purposes of redistricting.

The League of Women Voters of Virginia has a Redistricting Archive on its lwv-va.org website.

Virginia Public Access Project is a public interest group that promotes freedom of information and accurate reporting on important public issues, including redistricting, on its vpap.org website.

Larry J. Sabato's *Sabato's Crystal Ball* at http://www.centerforpolitics.org/crystalball/articles/ is a free, online political periodical that has commented on redistricting and will almost certainly include commentaries before, during, and after the 2021 redistricting session.

OneVirginia2021 is a consortium of people and groups specifically devoted to impartial apportionment in the state and has a website at onevirginia2021.org that includes very fine maps of current Senate, House of Delegates, and House of Representatives districts.

INDEX

Italicized page numbers refer to maps/illustrations.